Overcoming
The PERFECT
STORM

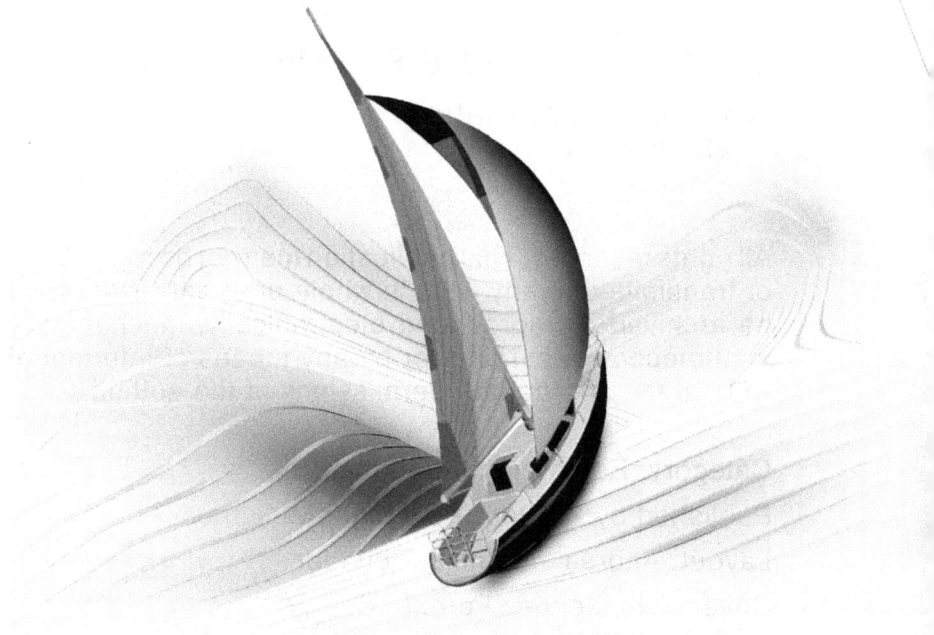

Ana Louceiro Plattner

OVERCOMING THE PERFECT STORM

©Ana Louceiro Plattner
1st EDITION 2024

Category: Restoration, Kingdom

Published by: Voice of The Light Ministries

Layout: Andrea Jaramillo, Ecuador

Cover: Ana Méndez Ferrell

ISBN: 978-1-944681-70-8

Dedication

I dedicate this book to my beloved Heavenly Father for His infinite love, to Jesus Christ, my Lord, my teacher, and above all, my brother and friend, and to the precious Holy Spirit who has held me and inspired me to write every page of this book.

I also want to dedicate it to my husband, Luis, without whom this book would be impossible. Thank you, my love, for every second, for every laugh, for loving and taking care of me always, and for being the best life partner in this wonderful journey through this dimension. To my daughters Paula and Valentina, I love you wholeheartedly for adopting me as a mom. To my Mom Ana Méndez Ferrell, for never losing faith, for each of the seeds you planted in me, and for persevering until she saw them germinate. Thank you, Mommy, for your love and dedication in helping me edit this my first book.

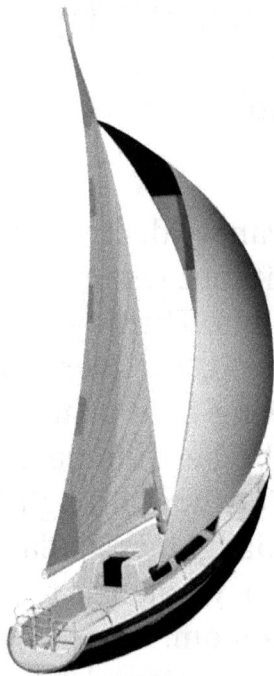

Index

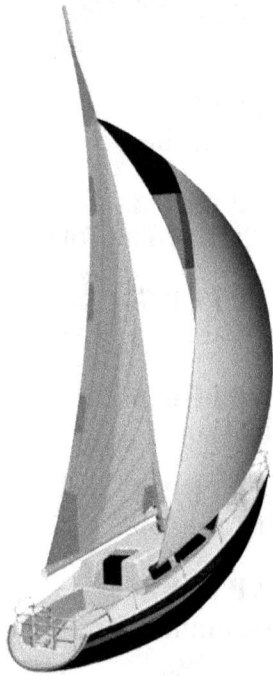

Prologue

By Ana Méndez Ferrell

In writing this foreword, I do so from the perspective of the ministry God has given me and not from a mother's opinion.

When I read the book, I was first struck by the phrase Ana uses to determine a truth hitting our society hard, "disposable marriages."

At the foundation of God's designs is that of marriage unity. Today, it is more an idea than a reality that has become a cliché without roots or substance and a subject that Ana addresses with great depth and understanding.

I was impressed by the unstoppable fight with which she clung to God, seeking answers to save her relationship.

The bravery, courage, humility, and perseverance of true love will lead anyone reading this book to reevaluate what true marriage in God is.

Ana takes us to the essence of what our Creator conceived within His heart when He thought of the wonder, joy, and power of being "One" as a couple.

Through nearly forty years of ministering to God's people, I have noticed how many marry "the ideal of love," "the dream of a fairytale union," but not the person. This means that marriage becomes disposable when the charm vanishes in daily life. The reality is that they were married to "how good they felt with that apparent loved one" but never really sought the perfect merging that melts the two into one.

For this reason, this book seems very important to me. God wants to redefine what modern society and culture have destroyed. Every civilization that fell apart was because it lost the original design of true marital love between a man and a woman and went astray in every form of moral perversion.

The Father's heart is crying out that we rediscover this design, and Ana hears it and gives us step-by-step the words and experiences that lead to the resurrection of a love that has died or is about to fade.

These pages you are about to read will touch deep places of the heart, be light where you no longer know what to do, and inspire those determined to overcome.

Over the whole earth, the power of love is strongly beating, which is the source of resurrection and is accessible to anyone who wants to bring their marriage to life.

The solution is to give value to that union by which they swore love to each other to the end and see in God the finished work of what they yearn for, as you will read in this book.

> " For then you will have your delight in
> the Almighty,
> And lift your face to God.
>
> You will make your prayer to Him,
> He will hear you,
> And you will pay your vows.
>
> You will also declare a thing,
> And it will be established for you;
> So light will shine on your ways."

Job 22:26-28

Thank you, Ana, for this book that is so propitious for this time. I know that many marriages will be transformed, and even those who are firm but perhaps without fire will find in these pages the light of God to shine again.

Ana Méndez Ferrell
Voice of The Light Ministries

A SHADOW ON
THE RADAR

I write this book because my heart breaks every time I hear that another marriage is in separation or divorce, and I feel within me a call for help. In these times of disposable marriages, split souls, and broken hearts, the Lord restored us as a marriage in a beautiful way and with an extraordinary purpose: to help others in the same situation.

If the Father could restore us to overcome the perfect storm and be a marriage within His design, He can also do it for you and your family. Indeed, if one couple is restored with the help of Christ and this book, it will have fulfilled its purpose.

Each relationship, marriage, and family are a unique and unrepeatable universe. God's perfect design for us from the beginning was precisely that: a family.

A man and a woman would be a unity in His image, and in that unity, they will bear fruit, multiply, fill the earth, subdue, and have dominion.

> *"Then God said, "Let Us make man in Our image, according to Our likeness; let them have dominion over the fish of the sea, over the birds of the air, and over the cattle, over [a]all the earth and over every creeping thing that creeps on the earth." So God created man in His own image; in the image of God He created him; male and female He created them. Then God blessed them, and God said to them, "Be fruitful and multiply; fill the earth and subdue*

it; have dominion over the fish of the sea, over the birds of the air, and over every living thing that moves on the earth."

Genesis 1:26-28

We are so far away from this wonderful design!

Each of us brings to our marriage the structures of the spiritual place we created to dwell in according to what we have lived. As we always say at home, how many unnecessary stones do we carry in our backpacks, imposing them on our relationships? Because, since we don't know how to deal with them, we carry them and take them from one place to another.

In addition, we live in a time when everyone has an opinion about everything, knows everything, and imposes their truth on each other. What is right and wrong, what you must endure, or not? Who is to be loved? We go through life making judgments without the slightest right to do so and, in most cases, without knowledge.

This book seeks neither to judge, educate, or establish any system or doctrine; it is a book of love. It is full of spiritual experiences and their dimensions. It is not a psychology book or a soap opera where we publicly expose our lives. This book talks about the storms of a fractured couple and how God restored each of those areas to bring us to a marriage within the Kingdom of God, full of His light and His life.

So, whether you are at the beginning, in the middle, or amid the storm, whether you have decided to stay together or not, this is a book of restoration, as individuals and as a couple, to become ONE once again, as you were in the beginning.

A "perfect storm" is a meteorological term applied to a specific and unusual phenomenon of great magnitude. In this case, I use it to describe an event in which a rare combination of circumstances drastically aggravates a situation.

An individual factor does not cause the perfect storm. It feeds on high and low-pressure levels, north and south winds, warm and cold waters, or the union of several storms, etcetera. The scenarios are diverse, but the constant is the same: we must have a combination of circumstances for a perfect storm.

Our perfect storm had lies, addictions, ego, selfishness, pornography, idealization, codependency, judgments, anger, seduction, deceit, loneliness, insecurity, fear, captivity, children, family, friends, and a backpack full of everything we had been carrying from previous relationships and the way we grew up.

The storm was a giant monster that thrived and grew from different fronts, becoming more destructive. When the waters finally calmed down, and we could see all the damage we had caused, it was so massive that there was no place to start cleaning up the mess.

Everything we had built was in ruins, and trust was non-existent. Guilt, anger, pain, our families and friends, everything, absolutely everything, was a mess.

The real work began when we decided to love each other without "buts," without conditions, with commitment and responsibility, understanding that we were two human beings full of flaws, of sin, and completely surrendered. Being aware that our decisions led us to the hell we lived in and that we did not want to go through that path again.

To achieve this, the change needed to be radical. Surrendering to God was the first and most wonderful step we have ever taken.

So, this is not a book for you to learn how to survive Little Red Riding Hood's big bad wolf. This is a journey into your soul to discover what it is you carry, to meet your spirit in the perfect design in which you were created, dying to yourself so Jesus can live in you. That is where you can empty your backpack of stones and begin to walk in the love of the resurrection, so you can return to the beginning, to the original design, and ground your marriage as God created it.

THE WARMING OF THE SEA

All things have an origin, both the good things we live and the circumstances we go through, as well as the constructions we do in life and the soul. In the same way, a storm does not form suddenly out of nowhere but begins with the warming of the sea.

We would all love to say that we have always made the right decisions, are never wrong, or have never suffered or experienced separation. However, all this is far from the reality we live in.

Why do we make bad decisions? Why did those circumstances happen to us? Why does it seem that some people live like "it never rains, but it pours."

To understand what happens to us in life, we must go into the beginning. If we do not understand the origin of our behaviors and situations, we will continue living in a "state of consequence."

Let us first understand that a storm forms, exists for a time, and then dies until it disappears. It is not something created by God to remain forever, as is the ocean, for example. Then, some things originate, live, and pass but have no eternity, and others were created to be eternal like us.

If we understand the latter, we will have a firm platform to watch the storms of life pass by without being disturbed or wreaking havoc. So, let's take a trip to our place of origin.

When I refer to the origin, I mean verbatim, the Genesis, how we were created.

"Blessed be the God and Father of our Lord Jesus Christ, who has blessed us with every spiritual blessing in the heavenly places in Christ, just as He chose us in Him before the foundation of the world, that we should be holy and without blame before Him in love."

Ephesians 1:3-4

The first thing we must be clear about is that we were in Him before the foundation of the world. That is, before everything you see and perceive in this physical dimension, you already existed within the heart of God. There you were created, and right there, within the heart of the Father, He blessed you and gave you ALL spiritual blessing in the heavenly places in Christ, holy and without blemish.

This is your design, what you were created for. Believe it, and then ask yourself: Am I blessed in Christ, holy and blameless? If the answer is no, we must keep looking for what happened.

I worshiped a few years ago during a Christian conference, connecting my mind and heart into a single frequency. I completely abandoned my will and subjected it to the Father, seeking only to worship and give Him glory. Like a science fiction movie, I suddenly began living an experience completely outside this dimension.

I was taken in spirit to a heavenly place, where I was before I came to this dimension. My shining self, like a small star, jumped and jumped from one place to another, full of joy and gladness, fluttered through the universe, while the tender gaze of Our Father looked at me and said with tenderness -"Oh Ana, never lose that joy of a child" - Ana! He called me Ana! That was my name! As the experience continued. I told him, "Father, send me; I'm ready," He repeated multiple times, "It's not your time yet; besides when you go to earth, you will forget about me." "Forget about you?" I replied -"That's impossible; I promise I will not forget you."...

It took me forty years to remember that promise. And I cried a lot when I realized that, as He had told me, I had forgotten.

Over the years, I told my mom about this experience, and crying, I described the pain in my heart for having forgotten that promise for so long. What I didn't expect was what she was about to tell me.

She said, "No, Ani, you didn't forget for forty years. When you were a child and just starting to talk, you came to me one night and said, "Mom, I want to see God."

- " With the lack of knowledge I had at that time and with extreme innocence, I told you: 'We are going to ask Him for you to see Him in your dreams. We prayed, and you went to sleep. "

The following day, you came crying to my bed at six in the morning.

- " Mom, Mom, I don't want to see him like that; he has open arms, and it's all full of blood; it hurts a lot; I don't want to see him like that. "

- "I was stunned," she continued. "I didn't understand anything that was going on. I was very impressed by what my two-year-old girl told me, as there was no crucifix in the house. So, where could my baby be getting such a vision? So, I told you, "Calm down, my love, that's Jesus you saw. He died for our sins but rose again and is now full of glory. We are going to ask him that you want to see him like this and not covered in blood. We prayed again, this time with more precision. The next day, again at six o'clock in the morning, you returned to my bed. "Mom, Mom, I saw Him happy! I could see God, and He was full of Light and beautiful."

My mother's words comforted me in the pain of having broken that promise I had made God, not to forget Him. But then, if when I was a child and barely had consciousness, I hadn't forgotten, what happened? Why did my life become such a mess?

The answer to this question has been the most beautiful, painful, intense, shattering, transforming, and powerful journey I have experienced. I found the beginning of the answer in what the Garden of Eden represents.

For six days, God created our wonderful home, carefully thought through, and designed every corner of our universe, finally putting the family He had made in the Garden of Eden. We were created in Him and set by Him into this dimension. Man had a wonderful relationship with the Creator; they talked and walked together daily.

> "And they heard the sound of the Lord God walking in the garden in the cool of the day."
> **Genesis 3:8**

Everything we needed to live in this dimension, our home, our dwelling, was in God.

Our Father did not want sons who would love Him because He said so. He gave us the freedom to choose Him, to love Him, and to obey Him or not. He gave the primeval couple clear instructions, and it was one hundred percent up to them and us whether we decided to be in Him and stay in Him.

"And the Lord God commanded the man, saying, "Of every tree of the garden you may freely eat; but of the tree of the knowledge of good and evil you shall not eat, for in the day that you eat of it you shall surely die."

Genesis 2:16-17

"Has God indeed said, 'You shall not eat of every tree of the garden'?" And the woman said to the serpent, "We may eat the fruit of the trees of the garden; but of the fruit of the tree, which is in the midst of the garden, God has said, 'You shall not eat it, nor shall you touch it, lest you die.'"

Then the serpent said to the woman, "You will not surely die. For God knows that in the day you eat of it, your eyes will be opened, and you will be like God, knowing good and evil."

So, when the woman saw that the tree was good for food, that it was pleasant to the eyes, and a tree desirable to make one wise, she took of its fruit and ate. She also gave to her husband with her, and he ate."

Genesis 3:1b-6

The reality is that the devil did not lie to them when he told them, "You will be like God," and he continues to tell us the same thing. The slight difference is that we become gods with a lowercase "g," gods without wisdom, gods without God.

Disobedience leads us to separation, to leaving our dwelling. We were designed to live in God and with God, but by becoming our little gods, we lost the perfect place to dwell.

Just as our body needs a place to live, so do our soul and spirit. If you want to understand how we were formed and what our parts are, I recommend the book The Spirit of Man by Ana Méndez Ferrell. In it, she explains in depth each element that composes us. However, I will explain and paraphrase what it means to be tripartite concerning this part of the storm.

You and I are tripartite beings; we are wonderfully shaped by our body, which you already know, our soul, that part of our being responsible for interpreting and decoding everything you think, feel, and everything that comes from the spirit, and finally, our spirit. The latter came from the heart of God, our eternal and powerful part, which, by being separated from God because of sin, goes to sleep, and the soul takes its place. The soul loses its ability to interpret what comes from the spirit and establishes itself as the new god and lord of our lives, and that's where the problems begin.

When we come to this dimension as babies and children, we can see and feel the spiritual world; it is normal for us because we have just come out of the realm of the Spirit of God. The most crucial thing in that early stage, before we start talking, is that everything we see and perceive of the Spirit is not cut off by a "that's not true," "stop inventing things," "you have a big imagination," so we live it and enjoy it while we can.

Then, circumstances, our parents, and our culture start to limit us, telling us what's true and what's not, what we can believe and what not, what's real, and what's our imagination. This is how the construction of our "world" begins.

As Emerson Ferrell says in his book *Resurrection Generation*, "The world is not planet earth, that is the physical Earth, the world, is the system in which you live and operate."

If we were talking about a computer, the Earth would be the hardware, and the world would be the software. In other words, the "world" is your operating system.

During the first six years of your life, that software will begin to fill with information, files of all kinds, with programs as essential as eating, drinking, and going to the bathroom, as well as the traumas that you may have experienced as a baby or as a child.

I, for example, have always considered myself extremely lucky because although my biological parents' marriage only lasted a couple of years, my brother and I grew up in the house of my paternal uncles and grandparents without losing contact and relationship with my dad and mom.

We were a big functional family that operated entirely difunctionally. I mean, my biological parents were still my parents, but they didn't live with us; they just came to visit, or we went for walks or vacations with them. My uncles and grandparents served as parents, but we couldn't call them mom or dad because we had those who were. Overall, they were and were not simultaneously, which was very clear and confusing.

Especially when you are six or seven years old, your classmates ask, why don't you live with your mom or dad? And nothing you answer will make the slightest sense, neither for them nor you.

In our house, if something was abundant, it was love. Each of the adults around us went out of their way to ensure that we had everything we needed. Although I always said to myself, "Everything is perfect," the reality is that deep down, I grew up with terrible traumas of abandonment.

At the end of the day, although I had a happy family that loved me with all their everything, for us in our hearts as children, our biological mom and dad had abandoned us in a way. From a very young age, I began to fill my "software," or my world, with limitation structures, rejection, fear, fantasy, and escape, among many others. It was as if each of these were a brick that I used to build the tower from which I would rule my life.

It is essential to understand that a child does not see the world from the point of view of reason. He does not know how to discern whether the whys of a circumstance are good or bad. Innocence does not understand that something is right or wrong. The child sees the world from what he feels; from there, he will build a dwelling where he feels safe.

I have always loved observing people and their behaviors, and I repeatedly wonder what it would be like if we could see the spiritual structures that each of us has built.

The bricks with which I built my dwelling were also influenced by the structures of my parents, my uncles, my grandparents, my teachers, and each one of the people I allowed to give me building materials.

When discussing what I had to live, I want to give you a graphic example of how we are building these towers.

As time passes, and Our Father allows me to help brothers and sisters in one way or another in their journey, I have been able to witness brutal constructions full of abuse, violence, fear, uncertainty, absence, rape, prostitution, hunger, ego, vanity, silence, abandonment, of forgetfulness and anxiety among many others.

I have seen real caves, even with bars inside, which keep them in frightful captivity caused by their circumstances and the brokenness of their souls, which the enemy sometimes uses to torment them, but not always. Most of the time, it is in the same abode where the punishment is. And why do I say this?

A large part of our soul's suffering is caused by what we say to ourselves from that tower we use to protect ourselves against the hostile world surrounding us. It is what we mistakenly believe us to be, where we feel less, where the whole world is against us, and where we think, perhaps, that we are not worthy of God's love. It is where we put limits and barriers to love and being able to trust others.

However, in the end, no matter what you have used to build your dwelling or the circumstances of each element, the vital thing here is to become aware that the place you built is not what God designed for you. That is the place that your little god, limited and scared, has built to survive in this dimension.

In other words, this construction is made by you and your circumstances. You created it from your limited being by the terror of reliving the same thing, to make you invisible, to protect you, to elevate yourself, to prove something, by the fear of not "being," to have a "safe" place in which no one can harm you, which is the biggest lie that exists.

These constructions create separation and individuality, but God created you and you came out of his heart to live in union with him, not in separation. You are part of a body in which we depend on each other. Later, we will enter the dying to the "I" to live in the "US."

If you live your life from that abode, from that construction, every step you take, every decision you make, you will make it from your **"state of consequence."**

Everything you have lived through to this day is going to have an impact on your future life. If there's one thing I've learned, it's that no matter what you've had to go through, once you return to oneness with God, and He becomes your dwelling place, then He begins to use all those circumstances for you to help others; They cease to be barriers and blockages in your life, and you become a living epistle capable of bringing out of captivity those who lived the same as you.

So be at peace; however, you came to your marriage, just like your partner. Know that the spiritual abode that you built, if you choose, will be destroyed so that you can begin to live in an unlimited dwelling filled with the love of God.

To get there, we must leave behind the state of consequence and start moving into a state of responsibility.

METEOROLOGY, TSUNAMIS and Low Pressures

A. | METEOROLOGY

Meteorology is an interdisciplinary science that studies the state of the weather, the atmospheric environment, their phenomena, and the laws governing it.

In our story the storms and the weather were something we did not see, much less, we wanted to see.

I met Luis, my husband when I was fourteen, and he was twenty-three. He had joined the "Forcados" group my dad had founded back then. For those who do not know what a "forcado" means, they are a group of fearless young men who stop a brave bull of 1000 pounds altogether with nothing more than their bodies.

In a very short time, Luis became my platonic love. At that age, he was everything to me—the one I loved to have and dream with, awake and asleep, yet was unattainable.

Luis was always very close to my family, a great friend of my dad and my brothers (apart from my brother, I have two half-brothers from my dad's second marriage and two sisters, daughters of my uncles with whom I grew up, for me, there are no differences between them or whether they are half-brothers or sisters-cousins; for me, I am the eldest of six siblings.)

Besides being a forcado, Luis, also known as "Pollo" (Tiny Chicken, for having blond hair), was the director of a popular disco to which we all were allowed to go. They were at peace at home that we would be fine since it was a trustworthy establishment.

So, his disco became where all my brothers went to party, and I could daydream about him.

For twenty-four years, we lived "the dance of mismatch." First, I was very young, and he was impossible for a thousand reasons. Then, when I grew up, he already had a wife and was soon to be a dad. A few years later, he separated, and now the one married was me.

When I divorced, I found out he had returned to his wife and was now expecting another child. So, I went on my way to California, where I had a torturous relationship in which I was psychologically abused and separated from all my family and friends. I finally managed to get out of it after that man put a gun to my head.

I was devastated, traumatized, and eager to reinvent myself, so I moved to Cancun, a beautiful beach town in Mexico's Riviera Maya. I knew Luis was divorced and lived in Playa del Carmen, which was very close. So, I sent him a message to let him know of my new whereabouts, and that I would be very happy to see him again, to which he replied: - "Don't tell me that! I just moved to Mexico City."

At this point, I cracked laughing; it was clear there was no way to match my platonic love. But a year later, a common friend died, and without planning it, without calls or messages, as orchestrated by heaven, one of my sisters asked Luis to drive her car to the funeral and to pick me up at the airport on their way.

On that painful day, we were together, and something finally connected. I returned to Cancun, and he stayed in Mexico, but the text messages shortened the distance and lengthened the conversations. He confessed he liked me a few months later, and I was frozen. Twenty-four years had passed since I had dreamed that he would say those words to me, and that day, they became real.

I replied that I felt the same way but that my feelings were not recent; he then said:

> -"What? But why didn't you say anything to me?"

> -"Well, because every time I was single, you were not, and vice versa, so I went my way".

That's how we finally started our relationship. A few months later, Luis, his two daughters, the dog, and the cat were living with me in Cancun.

From a young age, Luis had struggled with addictions; at that point, I only knew the tip of the iceberg. Nor was it a topic we delved into. I knew that his life had led him to excesses and that during several stages, he had stopped drinking, being the last sober period of six years.

After the separation from his wife and his life being in a stage of chaos, he hit rock bottom and decided to stop consuming alcohol. This time of sobriety led him to get custody of his daughters, whom he cared for and raised full-time. He was the prototype of the "Super-daddy" who took them to school every day and did not miss a play while continuing his work in the evenings as director of a performance center.

I remember asking him if he cared if I had some social drinking, and he said no, that he was used to being surrounded by people who drank, and it didn't affect him. So, I drank at the many parties and social events we attended each week.

Everything was quite fine until one day, he came home, and he had been drinking. I remember his words perfectly: "Now you know all my facets; this is my true self."

I had never dealt with alcoholism, nor did I have any idea of its consequences or how serious it was that he had drunk again. My instinct told me, "These are unknown waters; be careful; you do not know what you are facing." So, I watched him for a few days. He didn't drink alcohol for weeks, so I put my instinct to rest and went on with our lives.

As the months went by, we went out on a date, and he asked:

> - "I fancied having a wine. Do you want us to order one?"

> - "And how does this affect you? I don't know why you stopped drinking so long and why now you want to drink again. You know yourself, I don't; if you think it doesn't affect you, I'm ok with it."

> - "The last time I drank was that time a couple of months ago, and I had not craved it until now, so as long as it is like that, I do not see any problem."

This was not true; this was A BIG PROBLEM, which he minimized to be able to drink, and I dismissed it because I believed him when he told me that everything was fine.

This was the point where we should have had our eyes on the weather radar and be very attentive to every change in the water, in the wind, in the atmospheric pressure, and yet I didn't even look at it.

And we partied many, many times.

B. | THE TSUNAMI

Life was going better than ever; we had just re-turned from a family trip where he proposed. I could not be happier, and while living my dream come true, the weather radar continued to issue alerts, which were constantly ignored. Our parties were getting more frequent; hangovers were treated with beer, and it began to be frequent to "hook" the party of one day with that of the next. For those who do not have an addiction, this is already terrible, but for those who do, this is a death sentence.

So, it was not that the storm did not give several warnings on the radar, but in my world of fantasy, idealization, and perfect worlds, I never paid attention and was much less prepared for what was coming.

I was living the most wonderful dream; I had next to me the man I had dreamed of all my life: a little house with a white fence, two daughters, and two dogs. I hadn't been able to have children, so when the love of my life arrived with a sixteen-year-old and a ten-year-old girl, it was like landing in paradise, where everything I hadn't had was now there, a family like I had always dreamed of.

But ignoring the radar did not prevent the storm from arriving, so without warning, the tsunami wave rose, flipping over our ship and our existence. With a text message I read on his phone, Pandora's box opened, revealing everything he had hidden about his addiction and the darkness that came with it: demons, terror, fear, pain, loss, shock, uncertainty, and everything you can imagine.

Later, in chapter seven, I will delve into all the signals that the radar sent and that we ignored; for now, I will tell you that lies, deception, and drugs were only the surface of this wave that had come to destroy everything.

In an instant, the entire sandcastle we had built vanished at the mercy of this tsunami. There was nothing we could do.

Mistrusting and crushed down, I left him. I sought refuge in the hotel where I was working and moved there. The next few days were a dark nightmare of deep pain and disbelief that pierced my heart. I felt it physically as it penetrated my soul and even the depths of my spirit.

When losing a dear one, when we have been betrayed, or when we have lost everything rather because of addictions, bad decisions, or for whatever reason, the pain is indescribable. It is like an avalanche that connects with the past of all the heartbreaking experiences we never solved in the soul but only buried. They are dormant within us, alive, in the dark caverns of the heart, waiting to erupt like burning lava when it is under enough pressure.

On the other hand, the spirit shakes, the soul trembles, and our whole being seems to have stopped. We have a hard time making sense of conversations. We are in a lethargic state where everything seems to move in slow motion, like in a movie.

At that point our frequency is so low that our immune system falls, and our hearts, both physical and soulish break as if they were pierced by a knife that we can feel in the flesh.

It is in that place of despondency, of no strength, where we are so vulnerable and broken that we can raise our gaze to heaven, understanding that only God can move us forward.

That position of humility where we dare to look within enables us to see that control tower we operate from and make decisions to live in a "State of Consequence" until we determine to stop and change what must be changed.

If you have gone through a situation like this, you know what I'm talking about. If you are lucky enough not to have lived any of this, do not stop reading because understanding pain is key not to building a tower of insensibility.

This tower we built as limited gods is formed by each of the circumstances and people who have influenced our lives, both for good and for bad.

There will be bricks built in us that are positive and edifying and many others that come from pain, traumas, violence, or situations that simply no one should live. This determines the way we think about ourselves and how we react to life.

> *"For as he thinks in his heart, so is he."*
> **Proverbs 23:7**

C. | LOW PRESSURES

Pain is a very dangerous construction material that can turn us into puppets without feelings. This is why it is very important to understand this chapter so we can enter our design and surf the waves of pain.

The pain we have not solved produces anger, jealousy, insecurity, revenge, bitterness, a contentious heart, unhealthy competition, selfishness, isolation, and many other things that destroy any relationship, whether marital, family, work, or friendly.

When we go through a situation like losing one of our parents, a child, or a couple because of infidelity, or we wake up from addictions to a shattered world or any other circumstances that have led us to experience deep pain, it is as if were thrown into a stormy sea. The violent waves lash one after another upon us, not letting us breathe and drowning us. As we gain strength to get some air, a stronger wave hits us once again.

The first thing I want you to grab hold of as if it were flesh of your flesh and read clearly what I am writing to you is that you must know that these waves of pain amid the storm ARE NOT ETERNAL. Like the waves of the sea, little by little, they will become weaker and more spaced. Write it, memorize it, eat it, understand it: " The waves are going to be weaker and more spaced."

My mom taught me this when my pain was so intense that I thought I wouldn't make it to the next day, "The waves are going to be weaker and more spaced." Repeat it until you make it yours.

And when the wave of pain comes, know that you know that Jesus is there with you, that what you are experiencing is a wave, and that it will pass. Grief is designed for our soul to adapt to the new life without the person we love.

You'll have friends or family or someone who comforts you in those moments, or maybe you're alone; say aloud, "The wave is hitting, but it shall pass; Jesus is here with me."

> " Fear not, for I am with you;
> Be not dismayed, for I am your God.
>
> I will strengthen you,
> Yes, I will help you,
> I will uphold you with My righteous
> right hand.'"
> **Isaiah 41:10**

Confess with your mouth the way out of the storm. Jesus slept peacefully during a storm that was sinking the boat in which he was going. Everyone around Him was afflicted, living the circumstances of this world, but He was resting, He had fallen asleep. In that rest, in that boat, He is taking you. Lie down and rest next to Him and in Him.

> "Now it happened, on a certain day, that
> He got into a boat with His disciples.

And He said to them, "Let us cross over to the other side of the lake." And they launched out. But as they sailed, He fell asleep. And a windstorm came down on the lake, and they were filling with water, and were in jeopardy. And they came to Him and awoke Him, saying, "Master, Master, we are perishing!"

Then He arose and rebuked the wind and the raging of the water. And they ceased, and there was a calm. But He said to them, "Where is your faith?"

And they were afraid, and marveled, saying to one another, "Who can this be? For He commands even the winds and water, and they obey Him!"

Luke 8:22-25

It is there, in the moments of deepest pain, that we must protect our heart above everything, because from it flows the issues of life.

D. | BROKEN AND RESIN-COVERED SHIPS

The following revelation, I know, will be of great deliverance to many of you.

In our physical body, it is medically known that scar tissue forms when a wound heals after a cut, a burn or after a surgery.

This tissue we know as scar tissue is completely different from the rest of our skin, it is harder, it looks and feels different, and in many cases, it loses complete sensitivity.

The same thing happens to our soulful heart. Every time we go through a situation of deep pain, it's like being pierced with a knife, and that wound, like everything else, eventually heals, or at least, that's what they tell you in this world, but that's not true!

Time alone is not going to heal your wound, it is simply going to close it, and that piece of your heart, which you loved and enjoyed with that someone or something you lost, dies scarred.

When you have an open wound because of the situation of pain you are experiencing, the most important thing in that moment is that you give your heart to Jesus. If this is your case, touch your heart with your hand and say: "Lord, I give you my heart in this time of pain, cover it with your precious blood Lord, and do not allow any scar to form, only you and no one but you have the power to keep my heart intact. Keep it, Lord, in Jesus' name."

In those moments of pain, do not make pacts or agreements with pain, like: "I will never fall in love again", "I will never overcome this loss", "I will never be happy", "I am like a zombie", "No one will ever love me", "I am not worthy of love, nor forgiveness", etc. Each of these pacts or decrees you make with pain will make your scar bigger and deeper. I have seen cases of very dear people, who do not feel anything anymore and live like zombies because they made a pact with their lives and their hearts with pain and death.

This type of material builds impenetrable dwellings, full of torment, loneliness, bitterness, and selfishness. They become a true armor because they did not heal, this people did not deal with the cause of pain, neither forgive, they did not accept peace instead of pain and they simply filled themselves with scars.

When we are created, God puts in us a free will. This is the rudder of our life, a lever that we can pull towards ourselves, and be the ones who direct the course or who can push it towards Him and let Him lead it.

It is in those moments of pain when you must pause. When the waves of the storm give you space, grab the lever of your will, and hand it over to the Lord. Move it towards Him and may the flow of the Spirit, the flow of true Life, be what sustains you, be your place of peace and rest.

When you are amid that terrible circumstance, you do not understand why, as it can be a case of death. Do not lash out against God, "God why did you do that to me, I am such a good son, or he who was so good or she who was so young", "I who have been faithful to you and you repay me with this", etc.

Watch your tongue while in pain, for we are nothing to judge His will, much less understand it. Death is not that a person leaves this dimension, death is being separated from God. So never stop loving God and honoring Him above all things, no matter how deep your pain is. Don't separate yourself from Him, and end up walking dead in this life, wandering in this dimension, without His presence.

On the other hand, there are situations in which pain comes because of our actions.

Like the tares of seeds that we let grow, and that we do not uproot in time, and worse, that we have sown. Judgments came upon us because we were executing judges over those who harmed us. As Jesus Himself said, "Whatever man sows, that he will also reap."

Psalm 73:21 says,
"Thus my heart was grieved,
And I was vexed in my mind..."

In those moments of pain do not surrender to bitterness, do not become a victim of your circumstances. Pits of bitterness not only scar the heart but also dry it up. The root of bitterness can grow very subtly if you don't realize it.

In the Bible there is a character called Naomi, we can read her story in the book of Ruth. She lost her husband and children, and her bitterness reached such a degree that she asked her family when she returned to Bethlehem to call her Mara.

> *"But she said to them, "Do not call me Naomi; call me Mara, for the Almighty has dealt very bitterly with me..."*
>
> **Ruth 1:20**

Bitterness changes our whole essence. There is something that strikes me a lot about Naomi, she had asked them to call her, Mara. This word in Hebrew means bitter. After this confession that occurred in Bethlehem, it is that the love and mercy of the Eternal Father turned to her, and Ruth, her daughter-in-law, ends up giving her a grandson and with this, the joy of a new life for Naomi.

Confessing our pain and bitterness are among the first and most important steps in healing a hardened heart. Later, and in order not to lose the thread of the storm we were talking about, I will enter the path that leads us to complete healing.

E. | THE SHIP AT THE SHIPYARD

Up to this point perhaps what I have shared can be preventive, so that you learn it and make it yours so that you know what to do in those moments of intense pain.

But now I need to talk to you who have a heart full of scars, to you who have no idea how to love because you have been hurt so much that you do not even know how to do it, to you who have been betrayed when you had your whole life full of dreams and illusions and now walk through life like a zombie, without even knowing why you get up in the morning.

I need to tell you that as it says in **Revelation 21:5**

> *"Then He who sat on the throne said, "Behold, I make all things new." And He said [a]to me, "Write, for these words are true and faithful."*

So, I tell you today, that Jesus is speaking to you because he wants to give you a new heart, but you must let him do the transplant.

The only way to make a scar smaller is to open it again, so show up with all faith. Come in front of the cross, take a spiritual knife, and reopen that wound that you sealed with bitterness, with covenants of pain, or by cursing your heavenly Father. Reopen it, let out everything rotten that was formed inside. Jesus will be there with you, in your repentance, in your humility, and above all in your pain, exchanging that piece of broken and scarred heart, for a new one, full of joy and capacity to love.

Do this with every scar you have on your heart, if you must make a list and open one by one, do it, but do not let any scar be closed and full of pus and death.

By opening each scar forgive and release, forgive and release. Whatever happened, talk to that person who hurt you as if you had them in front of you and say: "I forgive you and let you go and you don't live in me anymore", "I forgive you and I let you go". Forgiveness is not for the person who offended you, who raped you, who humiliated you, who was unfaithful to you, who died and left you alone; The forgiveness you give them by letting go is freedom and life for you.

I must warn you, that this process is going to be painful because you are going to live again and experience that pain you had when the wound was made, but now, you have the tools that you didn't have when those scars were formed.

That heart of yours, which came out of the Spirit of God before the foundation of the world, will be reformed within you and you can begin to feel again. The most wonderful thing is that your first great love will be Jesus, and you will remember that love and that oneness from which you came, and you will give yourself as a teenager because your heart will be made new for the glory of Our Father.

Thank you, Jesus, for our new and renewed hearts, thank you Jesus for lying beside us during the storm, thank you Jesus for your infinite love for which you shed your blood so that we could become one with you and our Father. Thank you Father for your beloved Son, thank you Holy Spirit because you allow us to feel you, to experience you, and to have you in us, to tear down every brick of our dwelling that did not come from you, because from today I begin to build my dwelling in you and with you, to live in your design.

This part is vitally important to us that are married, we cannot build a life together, with bricks of the past preventing the flow of the Spirit, we cannot love completely if we are still tied to these bricks of the past, of pain and circumstances, we cannot survive the storm if we do not surrender to rest in Christ.

IN SAFE HARBOR

During the time we were apart Luis and I, and I lived in that little hotel room, there were some moments that changed my life forever.

I remember that while I was working, I was distracted from my pain, but when the weekend came, it was an unbearable hell. Absence, loneliness, and cyclical and destructive thoughts led me to much darkness. So, I did everything possible not to be alone and to avoid the pain I was feeling.

One of my brothers lived very close to where I was, and every weekend I went to see them and stay with him, my sister-in-law, and my two little nephews one and three years old. The level of love, understanding, and support I received on each of those visits filled me with life to survive the next week. I will always be eternally grateful for that time together.

I remember how I enjoyed watching my brother melt with love for his children, "what an extraordinary dad he is," I thought, as I watched him interact with them. There was one day when we were talking in the living room, and on the other side of the room my little niece fell; It took her longer to fall than it took my brother to jump like Keanu Reeves in The Matrix to get to where she was and take her in his arms. The first thing he did was see that nothing had happened to her. Then he comforted her while she moaned in that cry of a little girl with her face full of tears, which he cleared away one by one, continued to hug her, and held her in a love that reassured her until she was ready to continue playing.

In this dynamic she knew that she could play and discover her little world and that my brother's gaze would always be attentive to anything, to protect and take care of her if she got hurt.

That day I felt the voice of God go up inside my heart, and He said to me, "As your brother takes care of your niece, so am I with you." I remember crying with emotion as I felt His love and realized that indeed whenever I had been shocked in my life, God's love had been there with me to sustain me and lift me.

Another of those moments was a night when I arrived at my room, and I was knocked down by one of those waves of pain that do not even let you breathe. I remember kneeling in the space between the two double beds. Prostrated, I observed my life, and I saw myself completely alone at forty, without family, without a house, and even without a dog to bark at me.

I began to complain about my pain, why Lord? Why? Why did my parents abandon me? Why couldn't my dad on earth be with me like my brother with my niece? Why am I living this separation from the man I have loved most in my life? Why am I like waste material and when I get in the way or no longer serve, I am pushed aside? Why? Why? Am I so unworthy of being loved? Everything I had fought for and believed in or hoped for was non-existent, and I felt defeated.

During that pain and that cry of despair, I could feel Jesus sitting on my bed and touching my head, saying to me, "Can't you see that I'm here with you and I'm loving you? Can´t you see and feel that the one that goes away and separates from me it´s you?"

To those who have never had a face-to-face encounter with Jesus, this sounds like total madness, but for me, it was the first of many encounters, which changed and will continue to transform the course of my steps to wherever He wants to take them. Because Jesus is real, he is alive and although some find it hard to believe, he is there at their side waiting for them.

From that day many things began to change, the first was my decision not to separate myself from Him anymore. I decided that He was not going to be a support for me only when something hurt me. I decided that from that day we were going to live this life together, the good, the bad, the happy, the sad, the wonderful, and the painful, I was going to live holding the hand of Jesus.

> *"Trust in the Lord with all your heart,*
> *And lean not on your own*

understanding;
In all your ways acknowledge Him,
And He shall direct your paths..."
Proverbs 3:5-6

"Delight yourself also in the Lord,
And He shall give you the desires of
your heart.

Commit[a] your way to the Lord,
Trust also in Him,
And He shall bring it to pass.

He shall bring forth your righteousness
as the light,
And your justice as the noonday."
Psalm 37:4-6

I began visiting a congregation in Cancun called Community of Faith where I found a family in Christ. I joined a small group where every Wednesday 6 or 7 women met to share a book we read together. God provided for me a place where I could see Him through each of these people.

I started going to the women's prison on Saturdays with the church group. The stories I heard inside would tear the hardest heart, and yet these women overflowed with love and faith.

I began to take responsibility for each decision I made that led me to the place I am living in today. My eyes began to open and everything that I previously saw as a victimization or an inflammation of my wounded ego, began to transform into responsibility, love, and forgiveness. And the first person I had to forgive was me.

Another of the fundamental pieces that needed to be restored and made new was my "Image of the Father". I did not know fatherhood because of the way I grew up. I had no idea what it was like to have a father who would protect me, take care of me, who would make sure that I do not lack anything, and would be my home central axis taking responsibility to move us forward.

Who could have taken that figure in my life was my uncle, but my aunt and grandmother exercised a brutal matriarchy, however to this day he remains a father figure whom I always find love and unconditional affection. I grew up fighting for what I wanted, and I knew that if I wanted something I would have to work and fight for it because I didn't have a dad to provide me with anything.

So, I didn't understand what a "father" relationship was. How could I have a relationship with Father in heaven if I had no idea what that was? The book The Father Heart of God: Experience the Depth of

His Love written by Floyd McClung came into my hands.

Reading it, immersed in God's love, restored every part of me as a daughter. And Then I was able to have the most wonderful relationship not only with my Heavenly Father, but also with my dad on earth, with whom I had the wonderful gift of being able to restore, love, and enjoy his last months of life in this dimension before leaving with the Lord.

I realized that I didn't have to continue living in the tower of self-protection that my limited mind had formed, I was now a child of God, and my dad had a wonderful home for me, a boundless home where He was Lord of Lords and King of Kings, a home where I didn't need to control everything because He was in control.

Understanding the dimension of being sons of God and moving in it, changes our dynamics on this planet and the way we perceive all things. It also entails taking responsibility for who you are now and knowing that once you are free from the prison that you created, if you let your mind and your fear bring you back in there, it is because of your free will, your Father has already taken you out.

It is imperative in a marriage when you want restoration as a couple to first deal with each other's hearts, regardless of what could have happened, or which were the fronts of your perfect storm.

This time that God gave me with Him in that little hotel room and all the restoration He did within me was, without a doubt, a solid foundation to start walking again, now from the responsibility of each of my actions, and of everything that I by myself did to get to that point; because, although I was not the one who unleashed the perfect storm, I had to take responsibility for what I had contributed to the storm, and it had not been little.

THE PATH OF THE
TORNADO

One of the cornerstones of any relationship is undoubtedly trust, and that is something that was destroyed during our perfect storm.

When trust is lost, you have no idea who the person you are sharing your life is. Everything you thought was unthinkable, turns out to be plausible; who is this person? Who did I fall in love with? What is he capable of?

From one moment to the next you find yourself amid an avalanche of thoughts, between what is real, and those fueled by pain. Mental soap-operas are worse than any Latin American production.

Trust is one of those pieces that you give freely when starting a relationship, but when it is destroyed, it is one of the most complicated pieces to restore. However, it is possible. The process is long, tedious, painful and leads to situations that may even seem toxic and unhealthy, but the important thing is that they are not eternal. Over time, when trust returns accompanied by genuine transformation and deep forgiveness, you can breathe easily again.

As a Chinese porcelain bowl that when broken is restored with gold, when it dries, you can serve soup again, without fear of breaking or the liquid coming out, because this time, it is much stronger than before.

In our perfect storm the trust was absolutely destroyed, as a town after the passage of a tornado, there was nothing left standing.

There were lies accompanied by "I give you my

word of honor", which had no honor, text messages, Messenger, WhatsApp, sexting, a total nightmare of lies, entanglements and confusion.

I have to say that if I had not seen in him a genuine repentance, accompanied by a fear of God that I could see and feel, I probably would not have considered the possibility of starting over.

I knew he could fail me and lie to me, but not to God; And that was the rock I grabbed hold so I could face the nightmare of regaining and restoring trust in our relationship.

So, no, don't imagine that this is an easy process by any means because it's not.

A completely new area in my life was to face the world of addictions, because, although I smoked cigarettes for 25 years, I never entered the field of drugs, and when I drank I did it socially and never as an alcoholic.

Out of nowhere, when our perfect storm detonated, two fronts appeared loaded with a force that swept away everything in its path and were precisely that of drugs and alcohol in which the man whom I loved had sunk. One of the things that I had to learn, was that an addict will do and say whatever, to defend and protect his addiction.

So, to restore trust, we first had to deal with these issues and then, one day at a time, deal with whatever we had to deal with just for that day.

With addictions, also came something I did not know and that was "codependency". And you know what? I was completely infected with this "virus," and either I dealt with it, or it would end up eating me alive. This is an obsessive and compulsive attitude towards the control of other people and relationships, fruit of one's own insecurity. In my case, I was in terror that my husband would consume again, which led me to want to control everything. In Chapter 6 I will delve into the subject in depth.

On the other hand, distrust was at its peak, and was fueled by lies and the continuous moral decay to which drugs, alcohol, and codependency entail. If we add to this the social, work, and economic pressure, it undoubtedly becomes a category five tornado.

Within all this madness, there was also something inside the two of us that impelled us to fight for what was ours, to look inside our eyes and find the depths of our essence, where our love was still alive and refused to die in the storm.

Love does not reason, love will go far beyond what intelligence or reasoning can tell you. Love serves a purpose and is the force that will go against your logical arguments. It was the essence of that love that lifted us to fight together.

We were both on a sinking ship and we knew it, but when we decided to fight for our love, we both focused and put everything of ourselves to get the water out of the boat and sail into peaceful waters so we could start rebuilding.

Without this commitment everything would have been impossible.

A. | A GLASS-BOTTOM BOAT

This part was by far the most complicated, the most toxic and where literally more than once I ended up vomiting to get out everything rotten inside of me and the poison that I had that was killing me.

The lies and text messages that shattered all the trust in our relationship, were pure arsenic, and a torment every time he grabbed his phone.

So, for a very good while, phones remained unlocked and social networks open. All people with whom there was improper interaction during the storm were blocked, and they could never re-enter our lives.

I remember moments where the Latin-American soap-opera appeared in my head and like a psychopath, I asked him "Who are you texting?", then I grabbed the phone, and he was just talking to his brother or a friend.... It was horrible, and yes, I did feel very strange about myself, but every time I took the phone from him to see what he was doing, or who he was talking to, there wasn't a single time I found absolutely nothing wrong.

Over time that began to build a bridge of trust again. I knew I didn't want to be in a relationship where I had to check his cell phone or social media, not at all. But during those months while trust didn't exist, that transparency, that glass-bottomed boat, helped me to know that repentance was genuine and that he was also drawing water from the same boat as me.

When I had those attacks of fear, jealousy, insecurity, which were like flashbacks to pain, I always found in him, love, affection, understanding, and a genuine apology. He never attacked me or told me "You're a crazy toxic lunatic, what's wrong with you?" and to be honest, more than once during the healing process I had attitudes like that, and for which I also had to apologize.

Over time and little by little this disappeared, to date the phones are still unlocked and the networks open, but none of us care about it anymore.

LIKE WATER IN A RIVER

A. | TOWARDS COMPLETE HEALING

One of the decisions you must make to restore your relationship is to forgive and forget. This decision involves many parts, many dimensions, many depths, and above all, it is not granted and then removed.

This process is different for each of us, but it is important to live it if you decide to continue together. Truly forgiving is the most wonderful form of liberation I know.

Forgiveness has many stages, and it is very important to reach the deepest one, where it hurts the most. Ego, pride, and the lie of "self-protection" are terrible voices that will take you away from true forgiveness.

In chapter two, we discussed bitterness and pain. Now, we will delve into bitterness and forgiveness, which is where we reach whole healing.

At first, forgiveness is unthinkable, "I can't forgive this," "I'll never forget this." But not forgiving eats us inside and fills us with anger, bitterness, and fear of being hurt again. It is a pure poison that consumes the bones and dries us out from the inside, producing diseases such as cancer and others that end up destroying us. Sooner or later, the body reflects the condition of the soul.

> *"Let all bitterness, wrath, anger, clamor, and evil speaking be put away from you, with all malice. And be kind to one another, tenderhearted, forgiving one*

another, even as God in Christ forgave you.""

Ephesians 4:31-32

"Pursue peace with all people, and holiness, without which no one will see the Lord:"

Hebrews 12:14

"A merry heart does good,
like medicine,
But a broken spirit dries the bones..."

Proverbs 17:22

Bitterness does not appear automatically, is a sinful reaction to your circumstances. In this case, if you do not deal with forgiveness in your storm, you will be dealing with this root sooner rather than later.

It doesn't matter the cause of the offense and its background. If you do not treat it and heal it, bitterness can take you to pits where imagination will torture you, making you believe even in offenses that were never done to you. Bitterness is a way of responding, which can eventually become your way of life.

It becomes the lens through which you judge everything around you. As we saw earlier, it turns into bricks and mortar with which you build your-self. It is an impenetrable shell that rises to pre-vent God's grace and His hand on your behalf.

> *"looking carefully lest anyone fall short of the grace of God; lest any root of bit-terness springing up cause trouble, and by this, many become defiled;"*
>
> **Hebrews 12:15**

Along with bitterness comes self-pity, unforgive-ness, resentment, revenge, anger, envy, paranoia, and many other destructive attitudes.

Bitterness is the result of very deep negative feel-ings that took root. Nothing is more powerful to fight bitterness than love and forgiveness; these will tear it from its foundation and burn it.

B. | ENTERING THE RIVER OF GOD

Jesus is the water of life, who became man and forgave us so that we could return to the Father, to our beginning and end. If there is anyone who knows how to love and forgive the most terrible atrocities, it is undoubtedly Him.

Water has a power that transforms everything, corrodes the hardest metal, rots the strongest woods, and makes its way through the rock to produce life out of it. It can break walls and dams, and its persevering strength cannot be stopped. The waters of God are his infinite, all-conquering love.

The waves of a storm of pain become less intense because they lack the force of life, but those of God's water, when we enter them, become stronger and stronger until everything becomes life, joy, and peace.

Immersing ourselves in the waters of Jesus to deal with forgiveness has been key to the complete restoration of my life and our marriage. That is where we become ONE with Him.

> *"But he who is joined to the Lord is one spirit with Him."*
> **1 Corinthians 6:17**

We decided to fight for our relationship, so I knew that forgiving and forgetting were key to restoring us as a couple. Otherwise, our lives would become hell, and we would simply be prolonging the end of our relationship.

A part of me wanted to forgive, but another part was afraid, another was angry, and another was full of pain, so I didn't know how to start forgiving and forgetting.

It was clear to me that, from my flesh and soul, forgiving would be very complicated. But this verse in the first letter to the Corinthians opened me to an extraordinary possibility. If I am united with the Lord, I am one spirit with Him, and He is the most extraordinary teacher of forgiveness and love. Here was the most wonderful key.

So, every time I had a painful memory, I began to declare, "Lord, I don't know how to forgive, but you do. Lord, I want to forgive, but I do not know how; teach me. Lord, you who forgave me all my atrocities, teach me to forgive as you did with me. I often entered worship and rest and let the Spirit of Christ, with its cleansing and life-giving waters, gradually flood my spirit, soul, and body with forgiveness.

Putting ourselves in a position where we, too, are sinners, transgressors, and in need of forgiveness opens the dimension of forgiveness. The position of "I am the saint, and you evil one did this to me" or "I am up here, and I am better than you because you dare to..." That position of superiority and ego never leads to forgiveness, and frankly, anywhere. Being aware of the mercy that God had with us greatly opens the dimension of mercy.

C. | BURIED IN MUD, MANURE, AND ROT.

When you are in the storm and pain turns into anger, a layer made of mud and dung in the spiritual realm forms that trap you in a place where everything smells bad, and this is where the most frightening internal battles happen.

This mud feeds on everything you say in your anger; it is a pit of despair formed of quicksand where everything that comes out of your mouth is charged with wrath, and many times, you do not even mean what you are saying. You feel like you're drowning, and even though you want to get out, the mud pulls you and envelops you. It's where you humiliate your partner and make him/her feel bad, where you victimize yourself, where every situation that led to the perfect storm intensifies and rots.

"He also brought me up out of a
horrible pit,
Out of the miry clay,
And set my feet upon a rock,
And I established my steps.

He has put a new song in my mouth—
Praise to our God;

Many will see it and fear,
And will trust in the Lord."

Psalm 40:2-3

God can pull us out from the mud and put our feet on solid ground. Once there, we must wash ourselves from all the mud of anger, rancor, and sin we allowed to stain us.

We will need the water of life, who Jesus is. In the spiritual and physical sense, water cleanses us and brings us to rest. Shedding our tears, for example, is key so emotions do not get stuck inside us.

Weep all you need, and let Jesus be the one to shelter you and keep you. Thank Him for that wonderful crying design that cleanses you from within.

Don't get stuck there. It's not about becoming a walking victim, listening to heartbreaking songs, and looking for every opportunity to feel sorry for yourself. It's about when you feel the pain, let your tears run naturally, without feeding it, let it come out until you feel it, and then take a deep breath, wash your face, and thank God.

I recommend doing a physical act with a spiritual impact. Take a shower, fill the bathtub, or get into a river, lake, ocean, or any source of water that you have within your reach, and while you immerse yourself in those waters, cry out and declare how all that mud, all that anger, all that rot is washed away. Ask your heavenly Father to put a new song in your mouth. Ask your partner for forgiveness for everything you said, hug each other, and rest in Christ.

Having been cleansed and entering the longed-for peace, it is important to close the door or the deck to that pit of despair and determine that you will never fall there again. God can close those areas of captivity. At first, it is possible that memories come to you or even that situations happen that invite you to open the well and fall back on it. Remember that our will is the lever that can always be tilted towards Christ, so you remain victorious.

Of course, some are stronger than others. Some will overcome rapidly, and others, even if they do not throw themselves into the mud, may get some dirt by thoughts or words said during the stormy past. You must know that if your decision to love yourself and to run to the waters of Christ immediately remains firm, the mud will eventually become dust and disappear.

In our case, we even laughed when one said to the other, "Please don't go in the mud again." Each couple will have its own phrase in which joy replaces oppression.

Forgiving and forgetting means that you will let the water run and that the past will be past when you look back. Whatever happens, never keep a "frying pan with mud." And what I mean by this is that, unfortunately, I have seen many couples who go through storms and that, although they say they have forgiven themselves, one of the two always has a "frying pan with mud" in storage.

That frying pan in which grudges, manipulation, and victimization are kept and stealthily simmers, waiting for the slightest complaint from their partner to throw it to his/her face with scalded mud so it will hurt. "

False forgiveness, disguised as holiness, is useless.

I remember a case of a couple of friends of the family. She had a very aggressive cancer that constantly led to hospitalizations and terrible pain. On one occasion, we were talking, and someone brought up the subject of cancer, and she, without realizing that I was listening, said to her husband, "Well, you and I know that if I am the way I am, it is because of what you did to me." This couple had more than 30 years of "happy" marriage, and I write it like that because that was what they projected, but deep down, whatever happened, she never forgave him and used her pan of muddy poison whenever she could. She sat on the throne of victimization, who ended up killing her a few years later. He, on the other hand, sat on the armchair of guilt, where he endured all the poison that she wanted to throw at him for years.

A marriage restored in Christ holds no freight, no grudges, no poison, no manipulations, no guilt, no victimizations. The past is past; its waters are no longer there; the river has already carried them away. When you both look back, you see the restoration God made in your relationship, the rock on which he put your feet, and how He straightened your steps. All this is to give Him glory for what He did in you.

D. | ENCOUNTERING JOY

During every storm, when the waves hit hard, and at the end, all you can see is the damage it caused; one thing that disappears is joy.

> *"looking unto Jesus, the author and finisher of our faith, who for the joy that was set before Him endured the cross, despising the shame, and has sat down at the right hand of the throne of God."*
>
> **Hebrews 12:2**

This verse is an explosion of revelation and power when you meditate on joy.

"who for the joy set before him suffered the cross, despising the shame". Jesus obtained that supernatural strength of bearing all the sin of the world, despising "the shame that comes with sin " through the joy he placed before Him.

> *"The Lord your God in your midst,*
> *The Mighty One will save;*
> *He will rejoice over you with gladness,*
> *He will quiet you with His love,*
> *He will rejoice over you with singing."*
> **Zephaniah 3:17**

That delight with joy that renews us with love and that rejoices with songs is one of the most powerful keys to which we can access in times of pain, and they give us a supernatural strength to overcome what we must overcome in Christ Jesus.

In our perfect storm, when the waters calmed down and we saw all the damage, we met one day to say goodbye. When the waters are not choppy and you are not wallowing in the mud, you can see that person you still love, in peace.

I remember that afternoon like it was yesterday. The next day, I was leaving for Italy on a trip we had planned together before the storm. We talked, we cried, we laughed. There were no complaints, no reproaches; it was an afternoon of immensely happy memories. We decided that, despite all the damage, we preferred to keep the beautiful moments, and instead of going alone, we went on what we had thought would be our last trip together.

We agreed that, on this trip, there would be no talk about the storm; we were not trying to reconcile, so we were not looking to negotiate anything or control anything. We toured every corner of Italy, laughing and enjoying love without expecting anything. In my head, this trip was a way to end with love, an incredible story, something to keep in our hearts and move forward without resentment.

During the trip, there were no conversations about the future; we lived in the perfect present every minute of every day.

We laughed so much during that trip that we fell in love again, and when the last day and night came, we were in Venice, and I told him: "I have never been so happy. I do not want the pink cloud we are living to end," "Well, do not get off the cloud" – he said, " Tomorrow we can be happy too, and we will deal with things one at a time but don't get off, stay here in the pink cloud with me," and I stayed. After Jesus, this has been the most wonderful decision I have ever made.

So, laugh, go on vacation together, remember every beautiful moment you lived together with joy, not nostalgia, and laugh at each other's nonsense. Fill every laugh with deep gratitude to the Father for that minute of laughter you have together.

Thankfulness and joy raise the frequency of our spirit, quench the exalted soul, and allow us to flow in love.

IN THE WIND

Only Jesus is the savior, and you are not the savior of your partner or anyone.

Trying to be the director of the orchestra, the flight controller, or whatever title you want to give to someone who wants to control everything is not only exhaustive and brutal slavery but also a very serious sin against Christ.

Growing up without that provider and protective father figure, I became a true "control freak" or inveterate controller. Everything had to be organized according to my expectations so that everything would turn out perfect. If we add to that an inflamed ego at work, you will have a nefarious person. I was the great hotel and restaurant manager who had reached the top alone, unbearable, bossy, and with few friends. That was me.

As I recounted in chapter two, once I arrived defeated at Christ's feet, He began to treat and transform every area of my life with much love. Still, the trial that followed in restoring our marriage was uncharted territory for me.

Our relationship was rebuilding, trust was gradually being restored, and now we had to deal with the two monsters I mentioned earlier: addiction and codependency. I learned everything I could about these issues as he went to support groups and sought all the help he needed to get by.

Within my fear, my pain, and my insecurity, I mistakenly thought that if I managed to control all variants, Luis would be fine and would not fall back into consumption, which is not only a big lie but a real hell. On the other hand, when he relapsed, my codependency made me justify his addictive behavior, so the fault was of "the drug dealer, the friend so-and-so, the situation so and so." Always trying to justify what had happened to the "poor little victim." All this was codependency at full speed.

In the process of leaving the internal prisons that addiction and codependency entail, there were relapses, nailed to the mud, and starting again. But in this new restoration agreement that we had started, there was something we didn't have before: open communication.

His addiction was the fruit of a large and twisted tree, full of darkness and emptiness, and you had to get to the root of everything to be able to throw the tree into the fire.

Within my ignorance about addictions, my codependency, and how manic I was in wanting to control everything, we went through a super stressful and quite disastrous stage.

If I called him and, for whatever reason, he did not answer, my mind immediately went into the darkest hole; what if he was already consuming drugs? What if he saw the dealer? What if one of his "friends" gave him something?

If something got out of my control, I would go crazy because I thought everything would be destroyed again so that I couldn't make the same mistakes, I thought as I drowned in anguish.

The idea of "one day at a time" did not assimilate into the mental structure in which I was accustomed to operating in everything I did; I needed a plan with sub-plans that was perfectly predictable and organized. The anxiety of the future, consumed with fear of him going back to drugs, was a brutal hell.

Then, I had an incredible experience with God; one day, it occurred to me to go to work on skates, although I did not know how to skate.

When I started the journey, I thought, "It's 4.5 kilometers, and I'm already late." In my heart, I felt God say to me, "There is nothing you can do. You will arrive at the time you have to arrive, skating one stride at a time."

"One stride at a time? But ahead, there are ups and downs; there are parts where the pavement is not smooth, and I can fall; I do not want to fall," I thought. The more I turned in my head to these details, the more I lost focus until a tiny micro pebble almost made me fall.

"One stride at a time" kept going up to my heart repeatedly.

Then I understood that I knew I had 4.5 kilometers in front of me and that the only way to complete them without falling was to think about the next step and analyze the terrain, the ascent, and descent ONLY OF THE NEXT STEP.

When I was before one bridge from my work, I went through a puddle, and the wheels of the skates got soaked, and one skidded. I realized I couldn't go on until the wheels dried because they slid sideways back and forth, and there was no way to keep me straight. So, I had to PAUSE!

I sat on the grass, waited, and once dry; I continued skating until I reached the hotel, safe and sound, without falling and with a great lesson.

There will be many ups and downs in life, and you can worry and overanalyze what may happen in the future, but you will lose what you are living in the present.

Life is the union of millions of presents that come together one by one. Each is the result of the actions and consequences you took in the past, and the only way to live it is the now.

There will be times when, even if you want to take

a step, the floor and wheels are wet, and there is nothing you can do but pause, change the circumstances, and keep walking one stride at a time.

This experience was a trigger to get out of codependency and be a support for my husband in his fight against addictions.

So, from that moment, we take life one step at a time, one stride at a time. We pause when we don't know what to do, listen to the Lord, change circumstances, and live in an eternal and wonderful present.

On the other hand, the issue of addiction and my husband's process of coming out of it was also a way Jesus used to deal with me.

One day, I heard the voice of the Lord saying to me, "Get out of the way, because you hinder me!" This made me tremble. In my eagerness to love and help, I tried to solve everything so that the stress that would result wouldn´t result in returning to him consuming again, and far from helping, I was only hindering and taking the place of Jesus in Luis's life.

I lived my transformation process with the Lord in that little hotel room, where He used my loneliness, pain, and defects as tools to open my eyes and change whatever was necessary to give me a new life. On the other hand, while I was trying to control everything, I was preventing my husband from living his process, and I was standing between Jesus and him, so I had to ask them for forgiveness and let go.

Finally, Luis could live that phase of change and have a wonderful encounter with the cross, love, and forgiveness of Jesus. That's when the relapses were over. When that happened, I decided out of love that I wasn't going to drink any more alcohol. This was a boat we were on together, and it was one of the most beautiful decisions I've ever had to make, and it was not hard at all.

For me, getting out of codependency was a long and complicated deal. On one hand, it led me to deep stages of repentance and complete surrender to God. On the other hand, I had to deal with my insecurities, which I protected by enthroning my ego, and it had to be put under my feet.

If you have a codependency problem, many support groups can help you cope. Understanding that if you try to control everything to justify your loved one, whatever his problem is, it will only destroy him and sink him more, the faster you can become an instrument God will use instead of being a hindrance. Yes, as you hear it, codependency hinders recovery, not only of addicts, but also of the angry, the lazy, the violent, the unfaithful, the liars, the depressive, and add to the list the problems that your partner has.

In ministering to many couples, we have encountered the "devil factor" as one of the greatest obstacles to marriage restoration. What do I mean by "devil factor"? This is the case where the person with the problem refuses to take responsibility for his actions. All the blame lies with the devil, and his favorite excuse is that there is no minister of God on earth who can help him.

In cases like this, they go to every deliverance ministry that comes to mind. The serious problem is that the Church often does not lead the person to take responsibility but diagnoses all kinds of demons, including the ones "of High Rank."

This is when the codependency of the spouse shelters and justifies this diagnosis from which they can never be set free and will inevitably end up destroyed.

Most cases can be solved with the tools I share in this book. Jesus is real, and where there is genuine repentance and a true crucifying of our desires, habits, and sins, Jesus, the Father, and the Holy Spirit come with all their potency to restore. Where the light of the Most High shines in a contrite and humbled heart, there is no darkness, no demon, no power that can prevail. Taking responsibility for what we have done with our lives is a constant in this book that I tirelessly emphasize.

Half-conversions, aspirin God, and playing a watered-down Christianity will never lead to the victory you crave.

HURRICANE
"ME"

A. | THE PATH

Each marriage is a world, and each couple is unique, with different dynamics. It is not a machine that can be systematically replicated so that what works for one works for others. However, there are areas in our souls that, once resolved, we can leave behind to have a healthier relationship, full of love and life, within the design we were created, and enjoy the blessing of being a couple.

We live in a society where the exaltation of individualism is praised and encouraged. I am not saying that it is wrong for a person to have goals or dreams that they want to fulfill. I want to get at that when we decide to share our lives with someone else, that part of "I want" must evolve into what "we want."

That "we" may be full of individual dreams, but the couple shares and supports them. If we take a ship, for example, and each one sets eyes on different destinations, neither of you will reach their disembarkation point, at least not as you had planned.

When each one begins to row to their side, the boat stops advancing, and then each one applies more force to control the direction. So, the arguments begin, or the silences, and either the two get tired and neither arrive at the destination. Rather, one stops rowing because of exhaustion, stops fighting, and gets angry and frustrated, while the other keeps paddling to reach the destination.

In this situation, each one's "I want" got in the way of the other, and far from being a team where they find love, support, and strength, they find them-selves alone, fighting against a force that pulls them the other way, filling them with frustration. Whether you were the one who arrived at the de-sired destination or not, you arrived exhausted and unwilling to share it with your partner.

Phrases like "If I had been by myself, I would have arrived much earlier" begin to exalt the "I" and separate you from the "we."

Continuing with the ship's example, imagine mar-riage as a trip worldwide, with only you and your partner as crew.

Each one dream and those you have in common are points on the map that must be passed. That is, to chart the course. For this, the first thing you must have is clear communication of:

- Destinations of the Spirit (what God has put in your hearts)

- Common destinations (buying a house, travel, companies, etc.)

- Personal destinations (work, study, social)

- Increases in crew (children, parents)

Perhaps during the first years, you will realize that it will not be easy to reach the expected destinations in the time you had planned, or maybe you will arrive earlier. Maybe you run into a storm along the way and must pause and rethink the next destination.

For example, in our case, we noticed that the boat was not moving because it was heavily loaded. The payments of everything that "according to us" we needed began to strangle us. The ship carried more cargo than it could move, so we had to rethink what was necessary and what was not until we were light again to continue sailing.

Every time you must rethink a situation, change course, or drop goods, the most important thing is that the ship's crew, you two, put the "we" first. What is best for our boat? Raise all the panoramas, see the situations from all perspectives, and put yourself in the place of the other.

Now, when one of the two begins with the "but I want this," regardless of whether that "I" destroys the "we," it is when, little by little, each one begins to row for your side. Many times, one of the two ends up taking out the lifeboat and getting off the boat, and the other does not even notice.

This happens when dreams and life plans lose communication. The goals begin to differ, and the mutual agreement ceases to exist. There comes a time when you don't even want to share the boat and life with that person you loved so much. You become different people with different dreams.

So, talking until you get in agreement and taking pauses before big decisions and adjustments in the route should become part of your life.

It is important to understand that both may have different vocations or goals. The important thing here is that each supports the other in their desires and that neither of these implies the destruction of the "we." There will be cases when one of the two must sacrifice their desires for the sake of the couple or children. But this step must be taken out of love, in the power of Christ, and understanding the further design.

Jesus gave up all his longings as a person and as a man to fulfill the design that led us to salvation and glory.

> *Greater love has no one than this than*
> *to lay down one's life for his friends.*
>
> **John 15:13**

In this case, there is no greater love than laying down our lives for our partners and children.

For example, we do many "Cross checks," which is what a flight crew does before a plane takes off, and once everything is checked and verified, they notify the captain to take off. We do the same. Questions as simple as: Are you happy? Do you need something? Can I do something to help you? are as basic as indispensable, so any route is prepared for the trip. Doing this on time and answering sincerely often leads us to realize that what is obvious to one may not be obvious to the other, and adjustments must be made TOGETHER for the good of US.

During your journey, you will have thousands of adjustments and unplanned stops; that is okay; it's part of life.

Now comes the eternal part of the "we" and where the "I" does not fit.

B. | THE INVISIBLE ROUTE

The Kingdom of God is found when we stop clinging and striving for the visible and the circumstantial. Our victories and those of our marriages consist in knowing that everything visible is subject to His invisible realm and responds to the substance of faith.

"By faith, we understand that the worlds were framed by the word of God so that the things which are seen were not made of things which are visible."
Hebrews 11:3

" Therefore, we do not lose heart. Even though our outward man is perishing, yet the inward man is being renewed day by day. For our light affliction, which is but for a moment, is working for us a far more exceeding and eternal weight of glory, while we do not look at the things which are seen, but at the things which are not seen. For the things which are seen are temporary, but the things which are not seen are eternal."
2 Corinthians 4:16-18

A ship that lives in the waters of Jesus is the one that has Him as head and Captain, where love and fear of God reign every day. This will make you enter the perfect design of merging into one, as it was when the first couple was created.

"And the Lord God formed man of the dust of the ground, and breathed into his nostrils the breath of life; and man became a living being.

The Lord God planted a garden east-ward in Eden, and there He put the man whom He had formed."

Genesis 2:7-8

As you can see, originally male and female were contained in one being, Adam.

"And the Lord God said, "It is not good that man should be alone; I will make him a helper comparable to him." Out of the ground the Lord God formed every beast of the field and every bird of the air, and brought them to Adam to see what he would call them. And whatever Adam called each living creature, that was its name. So Adam gave names to all cattle, to the birds of the air, and every beast of the field. But for Adam, there was not found a helper comparable to him.

And the Lord God caused a deep sleep to fall on Adam, and he slept, and He took one of his ribs, and closed up the flesh in its place. 22 Then the rib which the Lord God had taken from man He [b]made into a woman, and He brought her to the man.

And Adam said:

" This is now the bone of my bones
And flesh of my flesh;
She shall be called Woman,
Because she was taken out of Man."

Therefore, a man shall leave his father
and mother and be joined to his wife,
and they shall become one flesh."

Genesis 2:18-24

In the beginning, when God created us, male and female were A single **living being**. When God brought us animals to be named, we were **one being**. Everything that was brought from what was not seen, was brought when we were **one being**. The "we" was an eternal unity with the power to activate everything created in The Garden. We had the power to bring things from the invisible to the visible, and because in Jesus, all things have already been gathered, that power is active again.

"which He made to abound toward us in all wisdom and prudence, having made known to us the mystery of His will, according to His good pleasure which He purposed in Himself, that in the dispensation of the fullness of the times He

might gather together in one all things in Christ, both which are in heaven and which are on earth—in Him."

Ephesians 1:8-10

That ideal help, that perfect crew to navigate Adam's ship, came from within that oneness. Then physically two were made, but she was still "bone of his bones and flesh of his flesh."

That unity is what we become again when we marry and the two of us become one again in Christ and with Christ. If you notice, the design is the same as in The Garden, two who are one, living and moving in God.

"Though one may be overpowered by another, two can withstand him.

And a threefold cord is not quickly broken."

Ecclesiastes 4:12

This is perhaps one of the most used verses in marriage ceremonies and probably the least understood.

During this eternal and wonderful journey of marriage, there will be times when one of you is not well, for whatever reason. Then, probably comes to your mind the image of a couple, where the strong carry the weak and wounded, trying to save the other from falling off the cliff.

Now, let me change that picture for you. The weak and wounded one is not carried only by the couple; it is carried by the couple and by Christ, who not only carries in his arms the weak but also adds strength to the other so that he or she does not get tired and faint, too.

Let's give another example. One of the two is angry and self-absorbed and does not come to his or her senses. The couple always counts on Christ to deal with the other's heart and arrive at the right reasoning. There are always two strengthening the union and whoever is faltering.

"Jesus has said, become passers-by"
Gospel of Thomas verse 42

I use this passage from the apocryphal gospel of Thomas because it not only supports God's thinking in the Word but also gives us great insight into our walk through this world.

Having Christ as the center of our unity, living in that "we" is the design in which we were created, and it has unimaginable power. So, in that unity, the great heroes of the faith who passed through this world became strangers and pilgrims. Travel light and attentive, be prepared for all the wonderful things that Our Father prepared for you before the foundation of the world. If you are already one of the lucky ones who remembered your origin, you will realize that this unity came from the very heart of God.

To become passers-by is to focus on the things of heaven, without attachments to physical things and of this dimension, because we cannot carry everything material.

To become passers-by is to walk in Christ and with Christ.

> *If then you were raised with Christ, seek those things which are above, where Christ is, sitting at the right hand of God. Set your mind on things above, not on things on the earth. For you died, and your life is hidden with Christ in God.*
>
> **Colossians 3:1-3**

Many others marry because they are in love with what they feel when they are with their partner, but they never join in marriage with the person, and when they stop feeling that first euphoria, they realize that they do not even know who they are married to. The "I don't feel anything anymore when I'm with you" begins when they wake up from that illusory lie. They married with a feeling and not with their spouse.

Others marry to have sex, to obtain social status, for convenience, or because it is simply what is expected of them, but deep down, they sign a legal agreement and never seek to merge into one flesh.

They live in an eternal "me" that leaves them completely alone. That "I" will invariably seek to control the other, to be right, and to do their own will.

Merging with God into a unity, where Christ is our head, completely changes the couple's dynamics.

Decisions are not made individually. When plans or decisions are to be made, they are brought to the table and weighed with love. You pray you listen to the other person's point of view and respect the final decision.

There will be decisions with which you do not agree; more than once, we have had to say, "I do not agree with this decision, but if you think it is best for our family, you can count on me," and many times things have gone well, others not so much. Knowing that no matter what happens, we are still one gives us the strength and peace of knowing that even if the choice was wrong, we will prob- ably end up laughing in a "I told you so", but not sarcastic, not with anger. A fit of laughter has of- ten followed them because when everything goes wrong, it's best to laugh, hug, and lift each other.

C. | THE ORDER ON BOARD

Now, let's understand a crucial part of this unity.

> *"But I want you to know that the head of every man is Christ, the head of woman is man, and the head of Christ is God."*

> **1 Corinthians 11:3**

This does not mean that the woman should be the man's floor mat, and he, being the "head," adopts a macho, dominant, and negative attitude. After all, in the same verse, we see God is the head of Christ. So, we can't think or assume this refers to a con- trolling role because it's not.

Here, we are not talking about hierarchies of su- periority but about order within ONENESS. If we go back to Genesis, before the fall, the two Male and Female were equal. When God took the wom- an out of man, He never wanted her to be superior or inferior to man, but she should be his equal in everything, for they were made of the same thing. God did not use soil of lower quality to create the woman, she came out of what was already created, of the same material, because they were oneself. The dominion and rule of the land was over both.

> Then God **blessed them**, and God said **to them,** "Be fruitful and multiply; fill the earth and subdue it; have dominion over the fish of the sea, over the birds of the air, and over every living thing that [a]moves on the earth."
>
> **Genesis 1:28**

Now, in Genesis 3, when man falls into sin, lordship first appears as part of the curse. If they had never fallen, they would have prevailed in that state of peace, harmony, and equality, which is God's design. Sin brought with it discord, control, and a government that subjugated women.

> "To the woman, He said: "I will greatly multiply your sorrow and your conception;
>
> In pain you shall bring forth children; Your desire shall be for your husband, And he shall rule over you."
>
> **Genesis 3:16**

Sin brought into itself all this separation, all this pain, and all this counter-design. This was a consequence of the fall.

The great blessing comes with the sacrifice of Christ and a marriage in perfect oneness. This returns us to the original design with an extraordinary variant: the Resurrection of Christ, which brought us back to the origin where "Christ is the head."

> "but, speaking the truth in love, may grow up in all things into Him who is the head—Christ— from whom the whole body, joined and knit together by what every joint supplies, according to the effective working by which every part does its share, causes growth of the body for the edifying of itself in love.""

Ephesians 4:15–16

In this verse, the image of Christ as the head of his body, the Church, defines the function of the head as the source of life and growth of the body: "Let us grow in all things in him who is the head, that is, Christ, of whom the whole body ... Receive the growth to build yourself up in love, just as it happens in marriage.

"But I want you to know that the head of every man is Christ, the head of woman is man, and the head of Christ is God."

1 Corinthians 11:3

The Greek word for head used in this verse is "kefaleh," and its meaning has no connotation of command or higher knowledge; "kefaleh" is generally used as a metaphor pointing to the origin or beginning of something. There is no evidence in Greek literature that "kefaleh" means authority or chief. (1)

"Then Jesus answered and said to them, "Most assuredly, I say to you, the Son can do nothing of Himself, but what He sees the Father do; for whatever He does, the Son also does in like manner. For the Father loves the Son and shows Him all things that He does; and He will show Him greater works than these, that you may marvel. For as the Father raises the dead and gives life to them, even so, the Son gives life to whom He will. For the Father judges no one but has committed all judgment to the Son, that all should honor the Son just as they honor the Father. He who

*does not honor the Son does not honor
the Father who sent Him."*

John 5:19-23

This relationship of oneness, of perfect love, in which we do nothing without the other and submit in love and honor, leads us to a marriage of Kingdom, of perfect union, of expansion, of Genesis. Because we were created eternal and creative, being ONE in God. We were created equal, and we can only return to our origins through that equality.

There are so many verses in the Bible where we can see the perfect design of unity in which we were created and the wonderful Kingdom power we have been granted.

A. | BE ONE

"For the husband is head of the wife, as also Christ is head of the church; and He is the Savior of the body."

Ephesians 5:23

This is an instruction for husbands about what it means to be head the way Christ is. He is ONE with His Church, and He loved her so much that

He gave Himself for her. To be "kefaleh" or head is to give ourselves in love and service within a relationship of mutual submission.

Let's read this in the proper context of the word "Kefaleh"

"The husband is the origin and principle of the wife, just as Christ is the origin and principle of the church."

B. | LOVE

"So husbands ought to love their wives as their own bodies; he who loves his wife loves himself."

Ephesians 5:28

C. | GIVING OF HIMSELF

"Husbands, love your wives, just as Christ also loved the church and gave Himself for her,"

Ephesians 5:25

D. | PLEASING EACH OTHER

"But he who is married cares about the things of the world—how he may

please his wife. There is a difference between a wife and a virgin. The unmarried woman cares about the things of the Lord, that she may be holy both in body and in spirit. But she who is married cares about the things of the world—how she may please her husband."

1 Corinthians 7:33 and 34b

E. | PROVISION

"But if anyone does not provide for his own, and especially for those of his household, he has denied the faith and is worse than an unbeliever."

1 Timothy 5:8

F. | FIDELITY

"Nevertheless, because of sexual immorality, let each man have his own wife, and let each woman have her own husband."

1 Corinthians 7:2

G. | HONOR

"Husbands, likewise, dwell with them with understanding, giving honor

to the wife, as to the weaker vessel, and as being heirs together of the grace of life, that your prayers may not be hindered."

1 Peter 3:7

H. | CARE

" For no one ever hated his own flesh, but nourishes and cherishes it, just as the Lord does the church."

Ephesians 5:29

I. | INTIMACY

"Let the husband render to his wife the affection due her, and likewise also the wife to her husband."

1 Corinthians 7:3

J. | DON'T BE ROUGH

"Husbands, love your wives, and do not be bitter toward them."

Colossians 3:19

K. | EQUALITY

"There is neither Jew nor Greek, there is neither slave nor free, there is neither male nor female; for you are all one in Christ Jesus."

Galatians 3:28

L. | SUBMISSION

"submitting to one another in the fear of God. Wives, submit to your own husbands, as to the Lord."

Ephesians 5:21-22

M. | RESPECT

"Nevertheless, let each one of you in particular so love his own wife as himself, and let the wife see that she respects her husband."

Ephesians 5:33

Submission is the fruit of deep love and uncompromising trust. Christ is a clear example of submission. He has his eyes on the Father, who knows that he loves him unconditionally and that every instruction he gives him is embalmed with the fragrance of that love.

Where there is no genuine love, there is authoritarianism, and submission is very painful and ends up doing a lot of damage.

The nature of a woman is to love, even with sacrifice. When she loves, she gives everything, she believes everything, and to submit to the one from whom she feels loved is a delight because she feels protected.

This is very important to understand. The woman was created with an instinct to protect her safety, vital to raising children as a bear with her cubs. The woman has, in her primal instinct, a radar against danger. She will do anything to protect what she loves against any stalking. It's the famous sixth sense they say she has. She sees the evil woman coming who wants to surround her husband and catch him, and while the husband has not noticed, she has already scanned the woman and her entire plan.

When a woman does not feel safe because her husband does not know how to protect her or her family, she will take the family's protection into her hands. This is an instinct, not a rebellion. This is when the husband must understand his role in the family circle so that everything is within the family harmony.

I clarify this because, with the liberation of women in society, we see that many husbands lie passively, letting go of their primary responsibility to protect and safeguard the welfare and security of the family in every way.

Mutual respect is also essential to understand because when this barrier is broken, giving rise to insulting and humiliating words, we break a divine structure that greatly sustains the marriage unit.

On the other hand, man needs to "feel like a man"; restoring manhood, in the sense of feeling respected as head of the family, is very important, not only giving a place to women. We must analyze whether we truly do this with respect, love, and understanding.

To be one in Christ, letting Him be the head, and to submit in love to one another is a gift given to us by the Resurrection. In no case does it mean giving orders or imposing the will of one upon the other. Much less does it mean having the other over absolute authority or imposing mandates as if instead of being spouses, they were each other's children.

These cases are extremely toxic and come from a parent's void that people try to fill with their partner. Men who marry and treat their wives as if they were their mothers, adopting a position of eternal children who must be smothered or comforted like little ones. In the opposite case, women who marry looking for their father in their husband assume the attitudes of a little girl with her father who spoils her in every way and who can treat her as a young daughter is treated.

In both cases, the roles of husband and wife are nonexistent and are marriages that cannot help each other as God's original design implies.

Returning to the subject of women, they should in no case be considered inferior, as is often taught in fallen and sinful worldviews. The woman was created from man, in equality. We were ONE being, and in marriage, we become ONE being again.

There will be situations in which you will not agree. In this case, the healthy thing is that one of the two has the final word, and by nature, it must be the man. When a woman takes on the role of authority, she lowers her husband's manhood, which God designed for family preservation.

There is something vital that I want to emphasize, and that is that we were designed to have different roles within the family unit. We are equal in terms of the value of our design, in terms of our honor, and in terms of our essence, but each one plays an indispensable role in the functioning of the couple. The man must have the pants and carry the loads and the responsibility of properly driving the rudder of the ship. The woman is the ideal help that makes it possible for the ship to reach its destination. She sees and understands everything the ship needs and has great understanding and intuition even to protect against the dangers ahead, while the man drives diligently.

The gospel of Christ is neither man-oriented nor feminist. In Christ, we are ONE in the complement of each other, in the equality in which we were created in the image of God. We are equally responsible for sin and likewise redeemed by the blood and sacrifice of Christ so that by the Holy Spirit of God, we may serve responsibly by making use of the gifts God gives us.

The Cumulonimbus

These are large white clouds of vertical development with a dark base. They are clouds associated with storms and electrical discharges, which can bring torrential rains, hail, or snow.

As for our navigation on the ship of marriage, these are deceptive clouds of darkness that rise in the heart when we have reached certain heights or when we feel that our social status gives us privileges over others. They make us feel that we are great in ourselves and better than others. They arise among different human races, in working life and especially in marriage. In them, they carry electric shocks that chill and destroy. They are haughtiness and arrogance.

A. | THUNDER AND LIGHTNING

"By pride comes nothing but strife,
But with the well-advised is wisdom. "

Proverbs 13:10

"Pride goes before destruction,
And a haughty spirit before a fall.

Better to be of a humble spirit with the
lowly,
Than to divide the spoil with the
proud.

He who heeds the word wisely will find
good,
And whoever trusts in the Lord,
happy is he."

Proverbs 16:18-20

The word pride comes from the Latin superbĭa and is a feeling of valuing oneself above others. The overvaluation of the "I" concerning others **is a feeling of superiority that leads to boasting of one's qualities or ideas and despise those of others.**

In the previous chapter, we established unity in "us," and this in Christ is what brings us back to our original design in Genesis. Then pride or superiority goes completely against God's original design for the couple.

When in marriage, one of the two begins to feel superior to the other, with arrogance begin the humiliations, the strife, the shouts, and the silence. Each of these are love murderers.

Violence does not necessarily mean physical blows to the face, but it is a whole system of control, nullifying the other until zero, and even less than that. Shouts and insults like lightning and thunder shake the heart and break it. It is like a series of giant waves falling, crushing the soul one after another after another, and there is no end.

Pride invariably leads us to the most terrible loneliness, both for the exalted who ends up doing everything alone because the other is a useless person who is good for nothing, and for the humiliated who no matter what he or she does will never be enough.

Pride and humiliation are terrible building materials that dry the heart, destroy the soul, and completely quench our spirit. But these do not start suddenly; they are very subtle; they make us believe that we are right and that our partner is the one who is failing. This means that far from supporting, helping, holding, or lifting our spouse – assuming that he or she is failing – arrogant judges humiliate, point out, and even disrespect and become completely intolerant.

No matter who is right, when instead of building, we destroy, then reason ceases to be relevant. When we begin to act as if we are always right and despise the advice of others, pride and ego have taken over the throne of our lives. Humiliating the couple, even with the simple fact of thinking, "he/she's stupid, useless, and can't do anything right," is the beginning of a cyclone that crushes and destroys everything in its path..

> *"For wrath kills a foolish man,*
> *And envy slays a simple one."*
>
> **Job 5:2**

Pride shows itself in many ways, and we must seriously meditate and pay close attention to realize if it has infiltrated our being. Look carefully and observe when someone wants to talk to you; no matter what the other person says, you want to be right and win all the arguments. In short, "You are wrong, and I am right."

The relationship is strangled when the dialogue ends, and the monologue begins.

In healthy communication between the two, there should be no need to win; it is about talking cordially, listening, and discovering new or different ways of thinking and feeling not only of the people you love most but also of the people around you.

You are not superior to anyone, and the sooner you realize that the less harm you will do to your loved ones and friends.

Insecurity is often disguised as arrogance to hide its true face. This is how fear and jealousy rise against truth and love, creating real hells.

> *"But if you have bitter envy and self-seeking in your hearts, do not boast and lie against the truth. This wisdom does not descend from above but is earthly, sensual, and demonic. Where envy and self-seeking exist, confusion and every evil thing are there.."*
> **James 3:14-16**

On the other hand, pride likes the judge's throne.

> *"Judge not, that you be not judged. For with what judgment you judge, you will be judged; and with the measure you use, it will be measured back to you. And why do you look at the speck in your brother's eye, but do not consider the plank in your own eye? Or how can you say to your brother, 'Let me remove the speck from your eye'; and look, a plank is in your own eye? Hypocrite! First, remove the plank from your own eye, and then you will see clearly to remove the speck from your brother's eye."*
>
> **Matthew 7:1-5**

I learned from my husband that when we point to others, God Himself points us three times more at the beam that blinds us.

What leads to substantial changes is the decision to leave that throne of "truth and justice" in which we have settled. Instead, seek humility in the heart and kneel at the feet of the cross of Christ, and in silence and wisdom, analyze what you are doing to contribute to the situation in which you find yourselves. Only then can we take responsibility for our actions, and we will see victory ahead.

In the same way that Jesus, with love and mercy, forgives us our most terrible mistakes and sins, these virtues begin to grow in us and build a new way of living.

The beam in our eye also represents the entire system we grew up in. The beams are pillars of construction on which it is built. Then, as we saw in chapter two, our view of circumstances will be determined by the abode from which we operate. If we do not remove the scaffolding, it will remain a rotten wood coating that will deteriorate our inner house. Beams are circumstances in which we fail and mistakes that make us mature. They are wrong ideas and worldviews implanted to form us and must be removed from us.

Pride, ego, obstinacy, and not being able to accept that we too are wrong and that we have a joint responsibility deeply separate and wounds not only marriage but our relationship with God.

Seeing our mistakes, asking for forgiveness, and loving from humility and not from pride will lead us to understand and build a true marriage of equality in Christ.

When we stop judging and imposing arrogance, we begin to understand that it is not about changing your partner to what "you believe" is the absolute truth and that is correct; it is about knowing and recognizing that we are two imperfect beings in development and growth who every day decide to love each other and get the best out of themselves.

Returning to the apocryphal gospel of Thomas:

> *"Salome says, Who art thou, man;*
> *from whom hast thou <come forth>,*
> *that thou shouldst lie on my couch and*
> *eat on my table?"*

> *Jesus says to her: "I am he who has*
> *been brought into being by Him who is*
> *equal <to me> I have been given what*
> *belongs to my Father"*

> *–"I am thy disciple."*

Gospel of Thomas verse 61b

This verse speaks to us of oneness, of becoming one with Him, and only then will we be filled with His resurrection's light.

In our marriage, the same thing happens; becoming one in which equality fills us with light and love as we were created. At the same time, separation, judging, and sitting on the throne of superiority is always accompanied by darkness.

Another way in which pride subtly begins to grow like a vine is that of victimization. The proud one surrounds him or herself with people who, according to him or her, are not able to do things well, so he/she ends up being the one who solves, who does everything, complaining about the people around them. This is nothing other than a mask of the ego, which exalts itself by seeking attention not only with the haughtiness of superiority but with the mask of the poor victim.

The spirit of victimization is very dangerous, it is manipulative and seeks to control through guilt, lies, and circumstances.

Control and arrogance make you believe that if you are not in control, nothing will go well, and things will not work out or go as you want. This is a very serious sin because we put ourselves to play the role of God, controlling everyone and everything around us, far from resting on Him and letting Him be the one who keeps us, provides for us, and takes care of us. We take that weight into ourselves, and that is not our design.

I continue to work on something because it has been a structural beam with me all my life: "If I don't do it, it won't be well done." That's how I was raised. I have always heard that I had to do things myself if I wanted to be perfect. This has been one of the most enslaving, annoying, and conflicting structures with everyone around me, including my beloved husband.

I have had to apologize many times for this structure, and every time I overcome it, I feel a wonderful freedom. I realized that this huge lie of my ego, so full of pride, all it did was saturate me with things that only I could do.

I was a slave to my pride, and with this, I was making myself angry and bitter and carrying everyone around me in this madness. If someone offered me help, I, in my dark superiority, would say no because first, they would not do it well, and second, I would have to do it again. With this arrogance in my decisions, I not only enslaved myself but also missed the opportunity to know new and better ways of doing things, doing them together and as a team, and freeing myself from the pressure of doing everything alone.

Leaving pride behind has been one of the most liberating experiences I have ever had. Despite all the work of forgiveness, repentance, cleansing myself of iniquity, and so on that I have done over the last few years, from time to time, it reappears, and I must subdue and crush it because I am not going to make room for it in my life.

My husband today laughs when I make a "know-it-all" comment that I shouldn't, and he says, "I don't need Google; I already have you," which fills us with laughter and me with shame for obvious reasons. Today, when one of us is wrong, we prefer to laugh together at our mistakes and get up with love. This allows me to ask for forgiveness, reconsider, and realize that I do not have all the answers, nor do I know everything, nor can I do it alone, and the best thing is that I am not interested either.

Life away from pride is light, and you live beautifully. Let us exchange pride and stubbornness for love, prudence, and much joy.

> *"He who heeds the word wisely will find good,*
>
> *And whoever trusts in the Lord, happy is he.*
>
> *The wise in heart will be called prudent,*
>
> *And the sweetness of the lips increases learning.*
>
> *Understanding is a wellspring of life to him who has it.*
> *But the correction of fools is folly."*

Proverbs 16:20-22

B. | THE EYE OF THE HURRICANE, THE ZONE OF SILENCE

"He who is slow to wrath
has great understanding,
But he who is impulsive exalts folly."

Proverbs 14:29

"A soft answer turns away wrath,
But a harsh word stirs up anger."

Proverbs 15:1

"Cease from anger, and forsake wrath;
Do not fret—it only causes harm."

Psalm 37:8

What happens when we get angry? In all relationships, we are going to have moments in which we do not agree, in which someone is wrong, in which things do not go as we had thought.

When we were in the middle of the storm, and the boat was shaking with waves of pain, anger overcame me many times. I have never been good at keeping quiet, and when I opened my mouth, only poison, pain, and wrath would come out.

I said many things that I didn't feel, things that hurt me and that I know hurt him, and I deeply regret it.

On the other hand, my husband is the opposite. If something bothers him, he does not say it; he keeps silent, often out of prudence but mostly not to enter confrontation. This way, it fills the pot with pressure until it bursts without control. This was one of the critical points of our storm.

As I told you in previous chapters, why did the storm come to our house without warning? Because of these silences. These were not the kind of: "I am angry, and I do not speak, and there is no dialogue," which is also a form of arrogance. These silences were, "I can't stand this, I don't agree with that, I don't like this, but since there are many other things that I like and are fine, then I better not say anything so as not to cause conflict."

As the years passed, the little things we endured while falling in love became intolerable monsters.

I remember one of the many conversations we had during the storm, in which I did not understand why he had never said anything to me. I felt deceived and living a lie. In my pink world, everything was fine, but in his, many unbearable situations made him escape and move further and further away from us.

These silences began to create an abyss between the two. The problem was that the only one who saw the abyss was him. I thought we were walking on solid ground, so when the storm hit, I had no idea why, how, when, or where.

Imagine a white house with white walls, furniture, and flowers, all immaculate and perfect, with a general taking care that nothing went out of frame. On the other hand, imagine a bucket full of muddy mud that had been accumulating for years in that silence. Now turn on a fan in the living room and throw the mud bucket on it. How does the house look now? Well, it's not so immaculate and much less perfect.

So, when we came back from the trip we did, where we decided that we did want to continue sailing together, this was a critical piece in our relationship, and that's why we decided to start with the well-known "cross-check" that we do all the time.

From that moment on, nothing was taken for granted, nor for sure. If I had the slightest doubt or felt that he wasn't telling me how he really felt, we didn't move forward.

The quantum leap was when Jesus came to reign as Lord of our lives, and of our house.

"But the fruit of the Spirit is love, joy,

peace, longsuffering, kindness, goodness, faithfulness, gentleness, self-control. Against such, there is no law."

Galatians 5:22-23

Little by little and with love, we found a way to speak without confrontation. One of the keys to making this dialogue happen was to change a major character flaw in my personality. Whenever someone said something to me that I didn't like, the fierceness of the lion jumped inside me like the owner, lord, and king of my jungle. How did I pretend someone would want to talk about anything with me? I had to take responsibility because I was the cause of the very thing that aggrieved me: their silence.

I needed to understand that my anger and reactions, as well as his silence, were just as lethal. Getting to the core of this polarity and undoing it changed the way we lived and interacted, not only with each other but also with family, friends, at work, and with everything around us.

We have both learned to speak with self-control, meekness, love, joy, seeking peace, and having patience.

Getting to this point was not an instantaneous process, nor overnight. Our entire identity, all the systems and dwellings that had governed our lives up to that point, now needed to be destroyed so that we could bring a completely different relationship to life. A relationship in which Jesus, the Son of God, manifested himself in a living and constant way.

When we come to Christ, the first systems that we must deal with and that the Lord deals with are the ones we carry inside. Like an onion, we must remove layer by layer to eliminate all the corruption and the erroneous religious and cultural foundations in us. Everything that was imposed on us or that we implemented and that makes us operate in one way or another, and that is against our design.

In other words, all the "software" added to the operating system needs to be restarted by the blood of Jesus. To achieve this, we must necessarily die to each of these structures of ego, control, pride, silence, disbelief, insecurity, fear, and other systems that we have used to build our dwelling places.

> *"In My Father's house are many mansions; if it were not so, I would have told you. I am going to prepare a place for you. And if I go and prepare a place for you, I will come again and receive you to Myself; that where I am, there you*

may be also. And where I go you know, and the way you know."

John 14:2-4

"Do not fear, little flock, for it is your Father's good pleasure to give you the kingdom."

Luke 12:32

"From that time Jesus began to preach and to say, "Repent, for the kingdom of heaven is at hand."

Matthew 4:17

"Now when He was asked by the Pharisees when the kingdom of God would come, He answered them and said, "The kingdom of God does not come with observation; nor will they say, 'See here!' or 'See there!' For indeed, the kingdom of God is within you."

Luke 17:20-21

In these verses, we can see how Jesus went to prepare a dwelling place for us, which is a dimension of the Kingdom that we can access and formed around each of us as sons of God.

The presence of Jesus in our lives transforms our dwellings. But to have access to this dimension, we must necessarily die to the system of this world that was overcome by Jesus's death on the cross. When Jesus rose, he resurrected us with him and led us to this dimension of the Kingdom full of life and the light of resurrection.

How do we die to these systems and this false identity? By releasing them and letting them go, immersing them in Christ so that life and the light of the resurrection may end with the dead within us to give light to life.

For example, in this physical dimension, if we decide to climb a mountain or run a marathon, we must hydrate to complete the feat. Without water, we would not reach the mountain's top or the marathon's end. Spiritually, it works in the same way; we need to drink the water of life that is Jesus Christ himself, read his word, enter his rest, let him and all his power transform us, and show us the areas that we must release and give him.

This is not an instantaneous process; it will take time. Dying to our ego and to our pride opens our eyes to recognize what we are in our divine design and identity and what is not.

Immersing ourselves in Christ is a priority so He can live in us, and we can die to the false identity we created. When it breaks down until nothing is left and all we are is centered on what Jesus says about us, we begin to live a new life.

For example, as I told you before, I was CEO of hotels and restaurants for twenty years, a prideful, organized leader, and blunt; they called me "The Thatcher" for being relentless and having been able to "be successful" in a world of men. This hotel manager, arrogant, with an inflated ego, full of vanity and self-sufficiency, ended up taking me to the most frightening abysses of pain and loneliness that can be imagined.

So, I surrendered at Christ's feet. Layer by layer, Jesus showed me each of these systems and dwellings, and one by one, with all humility, I surrendered them, asking forgiveness to those I had offended. I resigned from positions of high command until everything I thought I was was indeed destroyed.

Nowadays, when I look back, I have a hard time even imagining how I was able to be such an unpleasant person. I thank God every day for having dethroned the false Ana and given life to this new me, Ana, daughter of God, without any pretense other than to be a worthy daughter, Love Him above all things, and serve Him eternally.

> *"Jesus has said, 'Unless you fast from the system, you will not find the kingdom of God, unless you keep the whole week as the Sabbath, you will not see the Father.'"*

Gospel of Thomas verse 27

Fasting the world and the system's dependencies that bind us break their power over us.

Do you need to die to control or hand it over? Let other people decide and don't even give an opinion, whatever the outcome.

Do you need to die to ego? Ask for forgiveness, accept your mistakes, and humble yourself as Jesus did on the cross.

Do you need to die for pride? Start serving those you see as inferior to you.

Are your eyes looking outside the marriage for someone else, and your problem is cheating? Crush sand when it's sand. Infidelity is the fruit of a chain of thoughts that you feed until you end up consummating it. So, if you destroy a thought when it's an insignificant little sand, you'll never have to deal with a mountain. If you feed the imagination, the conversation, the masturbation, you alone are setting your trap.

Does your job bring out the worst in you? Quit! yes, quit! the world is not going to end, and you are going to start a new life.

Do you need to die to your reactive actions? Whenever you feel a reaction coming, say absolutely nothing. At first, this was hard for me; I managed not to say anything for minutes, then for hours; today, my reactive actions are minimal. I let days pass before giving my opinion on situations I would have taken ten seconds to burn Troy. If at the end of those days I still have something to say, I have already been so immersed in Jesus that whatever I have to say comes out of love with chosen words and edification, and not from reaction, and this has brought me wonderful results.

Are you controlled by money or lack thereof? I was obsessed with how much money I had, what I had spent it on, how I was going to invest it, and what I was going to use for the holidays. I had Excel sheets with detailed statements of every penny.

This was one of the most difficult structures to break. I had to lose everything, and when I say everything, I mean we went into bankruptcy. There was nothing to control because there was nothing left, and then my only wish was to be able to earn some money so I could tithe.

After desperately praying for a job, God told me, "I'm not going to give you any; come work for me." I was speechless. If God was going to be my boss, he would take care of my salary, and I couldn't have a better boss. So, of course, I said yes! I never made an Excel sheet again.

There are months that I do not know how we finished them or where the money came from to pay for everything we needed. I don't know. I only know that from that day on, my family's finances do not govern me, and my Father invariably provides for us. Everything that enters this house is tithed, and we can give to brothers in need and to organizations and ministries that are changing the lives of thousands of people. The more we give, the happier we are, which is an extraordinary joy.

Dying to money and the financial system has given us the most wonderful freedom.

So, whatever it is you need to die to, do it as Jesus did:

> "looking unto Jesus, the author and

finisher of our faith, who for the joy that was set before Him endured the cross, despising the shame, and has sat down at the right hand of the throne of God."

Hebrews 12:2

With joy always ahead, knowing that after death comes the life and light of the resurrection and with them the Kingdom of God and our dwelling in the place that God made for us.

To restore a marriage, each one has to die to their systems, work individually and together, and then, only then, you can give life to a new relationship filled with the light of the resurrection.

SUBTROPICAL
WIND

One of the fronts that can manifest in a marriage storm is children, especially if they come from previous marriages, as is often the case in our times. In our case, it was one of them.

As I told you chapters ago, I couldn't be a mom. So, when the love of my life came with two girls, one sixteen and one ten, that missing piece in my heart fell into place without asking questions.

Our first years as a family, as far as girls were concerned, were not only an extraordinary challenge, but they were territory without a map, a compass, or the slightest idea of how to surf waves that had never been part of my storms.

My husband lived alone with the girls for six years. During this time, he completely carried the weight of fatherhood, and in this dynamic, his eldest daughter took the place of the lady of the house and mother of her little sister.

When we met and started dating, I felt this whole picture was very sweet, and within me was the genuine desire to lighten their burden. Achieving it was another story.

The saying "Nobody teaches you to be a father" is known to all, and the reality is that it is true. Nobody teaches you. You are guided by instinct, by what you saw when you grew up. You eliminate that thought of "When I become a mother, I will never do that to my children," thinking that what happened to your parents will never happen to you, and then you make your own mistakes.

I want to share with you something I know will speak to your hearts and perhaps many of you will identify with.

Since I was little, I have been very analytical and observant of my environment and the characters who interacted with me. Something that always hurt me was realizing the pain in my grandfather's heart and the terrible relationship he had with my dad.

Over the years and many conversations with my grandmother, especially after my grandfather died, I was able to understand much of what happened very early in his marriage, and that marked his life forever. My grandparents are from a very small village in Portugal, and when I go to the village, I love to look for old family pictures in trunks. I found pictures of them in their twenties, where I can see the look of love of my grandfather and the nervous laughter of my grandmother. What happened to that love? That's not what I saw or experienced.

My grandparents had two children, my dad was the eldest, and Carmo, my aunt-mom. Before my dad was born, my grandmother got pregnant and lost that baby with the pregnancy quite advanced, which marked her deeply. At the time she became pregnant with my dad, her pregnancy was high risk, and finally, the long-awaited baby was born; my grandmother's whole life turned to being the mother of this precious child.

When this happened, my grandmother pushed my grandfather aside, and all the attention he got from my grandmother was now inexistent. My grandfather felt displaced, and his heart broke. His beloved wife was now the mother of someone who had stolen her from him, and he became someone in the background whose obligation was to provide for her and the child. This situation was accentuated when my aunt-mother was born a year and a half later.

For my grandfather, the culprit of everything had been my father, and this pain meant that they never had a good relationship. My dad grew up with a father who couldn't stand him, and when I was born over the years, my dad didn't have the slightest idea of how to be a dad, even less of a girl. A year later, my brother was born; my dad didn't even know where to start and ran away.

We must add that before marrying my mother, my father had just returned from Angola's independence war, where he fought as a soldier. Today, war traumas are called "Post-Traumatic Stress"; back then, you were just crazy and violent. My dad's case was no exception, and he had frequent nightmares full of horror and violence. During this, he even hit my mom, who did not know how to deal with his constant aggressions, so she sought professional help to heal emotionally and decided to leave us with my grandparents until her recovery. My grandfather, on the other hand, saw in this opportunity that place where to pour all those feelings that he had been repressing for years, and we overflowed each other in a love that I still feel today.

I saw this generational pattern of parents who do not know how to be parents break with my brothers, who, despite the examples of irresponsibility they had from their father, became wonderful parents, and that was something I had always wanted.

On the other hand, my grandmother and aunt-mother went out of their way to love and care for us. The problem was that they were both very strong women who established matriarchies where their word was the law, their authority was unquestioned, and no man in the family remotely had a say in the education of my brother and me. For me, it was normal as an adult and in the position of a mother that "my word was the law," so the breakdown with my daughters was monumental and undoubtedly part of our storm.

The first years with our eldest daughter were horrible for both of us. I had come to remove the place of "the lady of the house and mother of her sister." I was robbing her of the position she had created and ruled from in her teenage heart, and if she could not operate in these positions, she felt she was nobody. On the other hand, I wanted her to see that that weight did not correspond to her; at sixteen, she had to laugh and be happy and not run into adulthood, but no matter how hard we tried, we did not get anywhere.

On the one hand, I complained to her dad: "Talk to her; this can't go on like this. She has to understand that now things are different, and it's for her good." on the other hand, she complained to her dad: "Daddy, this can't go on like this, she has to understand our dynamics, why do I have to change them?" According to each of us, we had the absolute right to our complaint; the other was wrong and must adapt to the new life. My daughter and I were enthroned in our egos and rights, and we had no intention of giving in or putting ourselves in each other's shoes.

Meanwhile, we did not have a confrontation; all the complaints were made through the intermediary we had (my husband/her dad) because we were "well educated and civilized," according to us. Now, as we saw in previous chapters, my husband was a non-confrontational person, and he agreed with both of us until the situation became so untenable that everything exploded. And when did it explode? during the perfect storm.

Like a tropical storm fueled by a low-pressure system and warm waters, the relationship with our daughters triggered another front within the storm.

On the other hand, our youngest daughter came to me at ten years old; she looked like a cute little flea with glasses bigger than her face, super sensitive, and super spoiled by both her dad and her older sister. With her, we had to deal with her fears of not being loved any longer. Her questions and fears were, "Even though my dad has Ana, he still loves me? Why can't we all sleep in the same room anymore? They're not going to have children, are they? Little by little, with love and patience and sometimes even desperation, she understood that nothing and nobody was going to take away his father's love. Patience was certainly also one of the areas God had to deal with me.

When "The General" came into their life (that is, me), there were things that this family appreciated, such as order, structure, or knowing that when they arrived, whenever that was, there was a warm soup in the house. Professionally, I was known for bringing order and efficiency to chaos, so I did the same at home, although not in the right way. If I could turn back time, I would fill those spaces of militarization with much, much, much love and much patience. I would have loved to enjoy more of their childhood and occurrences, but I lived in the hotel working and only saw them briefly at night and on Sundays. I missed many laughs that will not return and that were lost in the past.

During the storm, this little girl suffered a lot; all her structure and stability fell apart, and although we reinforced thousands of times that whatever happened, we were always going to be there for her, the reality is that we took her into the tornado and suffered along with us the horrible storm.

The other polar wind I had to deal with was my mom, whom I judged for forty years for leaving us with my grandparents. During this storm, my mom was a key in keeping me in one piece. Not only did she leave everything to come and be with me and comfort me, but she also strengthened me in Christ and led me to waters of peace and rest where the pain, although it did not disappear, was more bearable.

During these months, when the Lord dealt deeply with my heart, I could see my mom's heartbreak when, forty years earlier, she had lived through her perfect storm. I felt her pain when her ship was sinking and to survive, she left my brother and me on a life-saving raft.

The intensity and pain of losing my family were so strong and intense that it opened a door in time that led me to my parent's storm. When that happened, I called her and asked for forgiveness. "Sorry, Mom, because I had been judging you for forty years, and like Moses, you walked through the desert looking for the promised land of your daughter's heart."

Those words and that forgiveness were so profound that they opened the scars of our pain, which were covered with the love of Christ. Since then, we have had an extraordinary relationship, which I find difficult to conceive today because we spent so far away so many years.

At that time, I did not know it, but restoring my relationship with my mother was key to destroying all the structures of judgment, arrogance, lack of forgiveness, and insecurity that I had within me. I was now able to start a new relationship with my daughters.

> "Children, obey your parents in the Lord, for this is right. "Honor your father and mother," which is the first

commandment with promise: "that it may be well with you and you may live long on the earth." And you, fathers, do not provoke your children to wrath, but bring them up in the training and admonition of the Lord."

Ephesians 6:1-4

Over the years, and with God working within us as a couple and as individuals, our family relationships have completely changed. When we decided to fight to get ahead, our daughters were key to making things work.

The first thing we did was to stop having a relationship with their dad as an intermediary. We asked for forgiveness, hugged, and allowed each other to make mistakes and start again. Each family member could be sure of one thing: that regardless of the storm or the ship's state, we loved each other deeply.

My husband learned to say what he thinks in love, without fear, without confrontation, always seeking the best for our family. If he disagrees or doesn't like something, he says it, and every time he overcomes the ghost of silence, we are so proud and filled with love for how far he has come and how much Jesus has transformed him into the great man he is today.

During the early years of our relationship, my husband and I lived in a free union outside of God's design, and while we were in that condition, we fought the worst hells. Little by little, as we were healing as a couple and as God was showing us everything that was out of order, we decided to get married and put God as the captain of our ship.

When the day of our wedding came, Pau, our eldest daughter, gave away her dad, and Val, our youngest daughter, gave me away. That day, Christ began to reign among us as a couple and as a family.

Recently, our daughters started their lives, careers, and dreams away from home. We were at peace as the time came for them to get off our boat, get on theirs, and start sailing because our ship had formed a guard port. That safe place where our daughters can return to rest, fix their sails, add links to the anchors, and navigate in deeper waters, knowing we will always be in the waters of Jesus' rest to receive them with open arms.

Nowadays, it is very common to find marriages with children from previous relationships. This topic is so diverse that more than one book could be written about it. We will find hundreds of variables; each must find the best way for the family to work.

In my case, I understood that my husband's heart already had three parts: his and the girls', and that every decision, attitude, or whatever I had concerning them was going to affect the heart of my beloved directly.

When I realized this, my interactions, decisions, and even my thinking changed radically. Everything I did about the girls first passed through the "filter" of my husband's heart. If, when I had to decide, I realized that doing "this or that" would hurt, then I rethought the solution.

I do not mean by this that bad attitudes or behaviors are to be condoned; I am saying that in any situation, love is always put ahead, so we'll find the best corrective solution in agreement as a paternal unit.

As a couple, we should never compete with or for the children because of "love." This would be completely absurd. Everyone has a place in the heart. The one who competes loses.

Talking about love and respect as the foundation of the family is much deeper than two words; it is a key to wisdom and understanding. This can help you direct yourself in many areas of your life.

THE DEPTHS OF
THE SEA

The perfect storm was behind us, and now the winds were peaceful. We got married, and our relationship with the girls increased daily. Then, the time came when God invited us to the depths of the sea.

To live in a state of responsibility, we must become aware of each of the bricks with which we build our dwelling so that we can give them to Jesus on the cross, as we spoke of in Chapter 2.

When Jesus died, he carried all these bricks, all this pain, all these circumstances as well, and the most important thing is that with the resurrection of Jesus, that light and that power destroy the tower from within.

We must understand that both the cross and the resurrection are not historical events that happened two thousand years ago but are spiritual dimensions that are alive and to which we have access and that we can enjoy. Being a generation that moves in these dimensions is already a reality for many people, and you can live by them too.

A few years ago, my life and my family changed completely. My husband and I had invested everything we had in a restaurant. We invited friends to partner with us, and finally, on February 28th, 2020, we opened the doors of the dream place. If you pay attention to the date, you can imagine that the restaurant was only open for seventeen days because, on March 17th, the lockdown began due to the pandemic.

A lockdown that we thought would last a couple of weeks extended until June, causing us to lose everything, including the friends with whom we opened the restaurant.

At home, we had already sold everything saleable; the credit cards were full, we no longer had money to pay our apartment's rent, nothing was left, and everything we had built had vanished.

Unlike when we lived through the perfect storm, this time we had God as the central pillar of our life, and although everything was falling apart around us, our family, our love, our center was firm.

My husband, looking for a solution to move our family forward, spoke with my mother's brother. He told us that the world situation also stopped his company but that he had an apartment with a car that he could lend us for three or four months. We did not have to pay anything, but the apartment was in Spain.

We prayed and asked God if this was the way He had for us, that the doors would be opened, and that all the procedures and expenses to get there would be solved and covered.

It did not take long for an airplane pilot friend of Luis to give us the flights practically; we only paid the taxes. We also had to make as a family a painful decision for the future of all, and it was to leave the girls for a while at their biological mother's house. With what little was left from the sale of the car, we packed our bags and came to live in Mallorca, an island in the Mediterranean, with the hope and promise of being able to get back together soon.

When you must pack your whole life in your suitcase and decide what stays and goes, every millimeter and every pound is evaluated very carefully. We included the book "Iniquity" by my mother, Ana Méndez Ferrell. I had read this book twenty years ago when she wrote it, and I had read it like a novel or a textbook, but something inside me called me to take it with us.

The airports, trains, and metro stations were empty. Few people were on the street or traveling, and the world paused.

Within that worldwide stop, a verse constantly came to my heart while packing our bags, while in the taxi, on the plane, on the train, and the boat (yes, we had to take all existing means of transport to reach our destination) and this verse was:

> *"But seek first the kingdom of God and his righteousness, and all these things will be added to you."*
>
> **Matthew 6:33**

The Kingdom of God? How do I seek it? Where do I find it? My heart is willing to do whatever it takes, but I do not know where to start, and I remember how important it is to have a willing heart.

> *"As for you, my son Solomon, know the God of your father, and serve Him with a loyal heart and with a willing mind; for the Lord searches all hearts and understands all the intent of the thoughts. If you seek Him, He will be found by you; but if you forsake Him, He will cast you off forever."*
>
> **1 Chronicles 28:9**

> *"Search me, O God, and know my heart; Try me, and know my anxieties."*
>
> **Psalm 139:23**

My mind, thoughts, and heart did not doubt I would persevere until they found it. I talked to my mom, and she wisely told me to work the Book of Iniquity, that it was important to cleanse ourselves from it and enter God's righteousness to find the Kingdom.

So diligently, my husband and I prayed together every day for three months. We began to read the Book of Iniquity together. We asked the Holy Spirit to show us everything wrong with us and our generations. And little by little, like someone peeling an onion, we went deep, layer by layer.

There were days when we could not advance more than one page; the Lord showed us how each of our sins hurt Jesus' body. Understanding this led us to a living encounter with the dimension of the Cross.

We wrote in a notebook a list of every sin and iniquity revealed to us; we searched and went deep into our being until we were completely naked before the Lord and each other.

During this process, there were no judgments, there were no shocks, there were no "that you did what? My husband's life and mine were on the table, with all their garbage and rottenness. We took each of these sins and generational iniquities to the cross.

Understanding the dimension of the cross of Christ as a living reality led me to deep, vivid, and painful experiences in which each of my sins was visible in His body.

The experiences were so real that I could see the wage for something I had done in every whiplash on his body. In every drop of blood spilled was my name, in every thorn stuck in his head were my unclean thoughts, and in his gaze fixed on mine was the deepest love, telling me, "Go on, I love you; I did this for you, don't stop now, go on."

These experiences with the cross of Jesus began to transform me from within. That seed that was Jesus himself within me showed me every day whether I walked in or out of his design and righteousness.

After having lived what my sins did to the Son of God, something was clear to me that I never wanted to commit the same atrocities again. The conviction of sin was now a reality in my life and my husband's.

From then on, every time we fail in some way because we are human and make mistakes, we immediately tell the other. Then we inquire what caused this fault because sin is nothing more than the fruit of something deeper. With love and patience, we learned to find the branch, the tree, and the root of things.

If we must fast for that, we do it. We carry it out if it is necessary to be silent and at rest. The important thing is to persevere until we take out any root that could separate us from Our Father.

We understood that the fear of God is not to be

afraid of Him but not to do or desire anything that can hurt His heart. This is one of the most wonderful revelations I have ever had.

God is love in all its expressions; even when he disciplines us, he does it with love.

We were exhausted when we finished looking for any sin or iniquity in us. It had been three months in which we cried a lot and experienced very powerful deliverances, even from curses that had been anchored to our generations for centuries.

At that time, we met weekly with our virtual church, "God's Workshop," led by my aunt Cecilia Blanchet Pezet. That day, she shared about Abraham and Isaac, a Bible story in which God asks Abraham to give him his son as a sacrifice. Abraham, in obedience, took Isaac to the mountain, bound him, and put him on a stone to kill him. When he raised the knife and, with his heart, handed it to his Creator, the bleating of a lamb caught in a bush was heard, and the voice of heaven like thunder broke forth to him, saying: Stop! God provided the burnt offering and saved Isaac's life.

As my aunt Cecilia spoke, something inside me began to break, and I began to feel God asking me to give him what I loved most: my family. I remember I couldn't stop crying. How come, after everything we went through, the Lord wants me to give him my family? What does this mean? I wondered; it was all very confusing. My crying was heartbreaking; my husband didn't even know what to say to me.

Then I had the most serious and difficult conversation with God I could ever imagine I could have, I said with all my heart:

> "Lord, I know that message was for me. You want me to give you my family, and I stand at your feet to give it to you now. I do not know how or what you decide to do with us. If it is your will that we stop breathing, so be it. Whatever you decide is fine; I give you, my family."

I was having a conversation with God, with God! Knowing that He has all the power to make us disappear in a second, He is the one who gives breath and extinguishes it. Everything inside me was falling apart. I could hardly sleep, and I would get up and touch my husband; I didn't know if he was alive or not, and as crazy as what I'm describing sounds, that's what I experienced: the death of my family.

When dawn broke, and we were all alive, my heart was filled with joy. I sang, I cried with joy, I gave thanks, and then I realized that something had changed. Before that night, the first place in my life was held by my husband and my daughters, and now it was occupied by God.

I hear many people say that God is the most important thing in their lives, and we say it too, but deep down, until we give what we love most, God will never have preeminence in our lives.

This is a fundamental principle for God to take the rutter of our ship; otherwise, life and marriage will be a constant struggle between God and us for control of the ship.

> *"For whoever desires to save his life will lose it, but whoever loses his life for My sake will find it."*
> **Matthew 16:25**

In other words, what we want to safeguard in our strength, we lose, and what we give to God, giving it up for lost in the heart, we gain eternally. We know we've given it to him because it feels like mourning a real death.

I remember that morning we went jogging by the beach, as usual.

When we were about to finish, I heard a voice inside me, which rose to my heart and told me, "Immerse yourself, immerse yourself." I knew that was God speaking to me. It was early November, and it was very cold, but the voice was so clear that I took off my tennis shoes and ran to the sea.

I crossed the sand, but before reaching the water, there were about three meters full of rotten sargassum. When I saw it, I was very disgusted to think that I had to sink my feet in that filth. The voice inside me was accentuated: "Go forward, do not stop; what you see is iniquity." I went into those black algae and slugs that reached the middle of my legs. It was disgusting.

I finally entered the water, which was so icy that you felt knives in your bones. The voice was getting louder and louder: "Keep moving forward, dive in."

When the water reached my waist, I let myself fall backward, completely submerging myself. Time stopped, and the temperature ceased to be relevant; those waters in which I immersed myself were not the frozen Mediterranean; they were the waters of Jesus; they were waters of life. Three times, I went out for air, and three times, the Spirit immersed me. When I went out for the third time, it was like being born again, and in my heart, I heard His voice again, "You are my beloved daughter." I couldn't stop crying.

When I finally returned to this dimension, I looked up to look for my husband and saw him about three hundred meters to my right, also diving into the water. The Father had called us both without agreeing, without religion, without systems, without repeating prayers. We had been baptized by Him, by His water and His Spirit. The joy and gladness in my heart were unparalleled, and I knew that our lives would never be the same again.

When I came out of the water, in front of me again was the mountain of rotten sargassum, and the voice, now in a cheerful tone and with a smile, said to me, "Will you sink again in sin and iniquity?" I will not!!!, exclaiming emphatically. I then walked to a place where I could jump it and laughed; I laughed a lot! I was filled with the joy of the Father, and I ran to my husband to tell him about my experience, and he told me about his. That day is recorded, and I live it in eternity, and every time I want to feel it, I return to it.

Having gone through the whole process of cleansing from sin and iniquity, as well as baptism and the new birth, destroyed the dwellings we build. This is how we move from living in a state of consequence and victimization to a state of life and responsibility, which carries the life and light of the resurrection in every area of our lives. We are no longer victims of our circumstances but children with a new life.

Little by little, we have been paying the debts that remained after bankruptcy and bad decisions. With faith and love, we know that the day will come when they will all be paid to give glory to God since everything we have today is by his grace and not by our effort.

FROM THE STORM
TO GARDEN
THE

No doubt, the road to the restoration of a marriage is a long one full of different circumstances. There will be good days, others not so much, but know that you know that, during the journey, you will not be alone; Jesus will take you both by the hand and into His heart.

As I told you throughout the previous chapters, to restore the couple, we must certainly work with Christ in ourselves as individuals. If we begin to live in the light of the resurrection and in all the victories that Jesus won for us on the Cross, we will begin to live a Kingdom life in which we will become one as a married couple.

But what was marriage like originally? Let's return to the basics we discussed in chapter 6.

> *"And the Lord God formed man of the dust of the ground, and breathed into his nostrils the breath of life; and man became a living being. The Lord God planted a garden eastward in Eden, and there He put the man whom He had formed. And out of the ground the Lord God made every tree grow that is pleasant to the sight and good for food. The tree of life was also in the midst of the garden, and the tree of the knowledge of good and evil."*
>
> **Genesis 2:7-9**

As we saw earlier, when God created us and put us in the garden, we were ONE living being.

"Then the Lord God took [a]the man and put him in the garden of Eden to tend and keep it.."

Genesis 2:15

He put us in the garden to tend and keep in that oneness of being. Work and protection belonged to both of us, who were ONE being.

"And the Lord God said, "It is not good that man should be alone; I will make him a helper comparable to him." Out of the ground the Lord God formed every beast of the field and every bird of the air, and brought them to [a] Adam to see what he would call them. And whatever Adam called each living creature, that was its name. So Adam gave names to all cattle, to the birds of the air, and every beast of the field. But for Adam, there was not found a helper comparable to him. "

Genesis 2:18-20

When God formed all animals to help them in their mission and gave them the ability to bring them from the invisible to the visible by naming them, they were ONE being.

"And the Lord God caused a deep sleep to fall on Adam, and he slept, and He took one of his ribs, and closed the flesh in its place. Then the rib which the Lord God had taken from man He [a]made into a woman, and He brought her to the man.

And Adam said:
" This is now bone of my bones
And flesh of my flesh;
She shall be called Woman,
Because she was taken out of [c]Man."

Genesis 2:21-23

God chose the rib out of all the bones in the body, out of all the organs we have, and out of all the possible options.

He could have taken a piece of the femur, the longest and strongest bone in the body, so that we would "walk together." He could have taken a piece of the skull so that our ideas were equal. Or perhaps he could have taken a bone from the hand so that we would get up and work together and hand in hand, yet God chose the rib.

The main function of the rib is the protection of the heart.

Pause and meditate on this.

You can amputate a man's legs and arms; you can even take away some organs, but he cannot live without a heart.

In her book " *The Spirit of Man*" Ana Méndez Ferrell (my mother) describes the heart in the following way, and I quote her verbatim:

" *The heart is one of the most important parts, as it is the center of our being and the main door to the spirit. It is the organ that determines all that we are and the realization of our destiny on this Earth and in eternity. The heart determines who we are, how we behave, and where we make every decision in our lives.*"

> "*Keep your heart with all diligence, For out of it spring the issues of life.*"
> **Proverbs 4:23**

> " *For as he thinks in his heart, so is he.*"
> **Proverbs 23:7**

To till and guard the garden, we can make thousands of agreements in our marriage and decide together who is going to do what. There is no rule, no system. Each of us is unique, with wonderful virtues created in God's heart to care for and love each other.

He gave a special purpose to the woman, the "Ishshah," by caring for and protecting her husband's heart. When the heart is cared for and protected in love, it is impelled to do wonderful feats.

" The heart makes us take the big steps in life. It is where the strength of our being is found to achieve victory, overcome tribulations, and take a risk. It is where courage and fear are forged and are decisive for our health."

What a wonderful, priceless purpose to protect our man's heart, our Ish.

> *" Jesus has said: when you make the two one, you will become sons of man, and when you say to the mountain, 'Mountain, Move away! It will move."*

The Gospel of Thomas, verse 106

Thus, united as one flesh, with Christ, and in Christ, we were put in the Garden of Eden.

> *"Thus says the Lord God: "I will take also one of the highest branches of the high cedar and set it out. I will crop off*

from the topmost of its young twigs a tender one and will plant it on a high and prominent mountain.

On the mountain height of Israel, I will plant it; and it will bring forth boughs, and bear fruit, and be a majestic cedar. Under it will dwell birds of every sort; in the shadow of its branches, they will dwell.

And all the trees of the field shall know that I, the Lord, have brought down the high tree and exalted the low tree, dried up the green tree and made the dry tree flourish; I, the Lord, have spoken and have done it."

Ezekiel 17:22-24

The time has come to till and guard the garden. The heavens are opening, and the Lord is shaking and entering like a hurricane to tear apart the structures and systems of this world. A new page opens in your marriage travel log. A page for those who are ready, those who are not lukewarm, those who are not afraid to rise, so that God's mighty and beautiful name is the only exalted thing.

The generation of the male Son, which we see born of the woman in the book of Revelation, which governs the nations with a rod of iron, the generation of the sons of the resurrection, the generation of the sons of light who are ready to raise their voices, is the generation taken from the bud of that cedar planted by our Father on the high and sublime mountain. It is the generation that understands how marriage is founded to bear fruit, govern, and subdue the earth..

A. | SEED AND GERMINATION:

When we receive Jesus into our hearts, a seed of salvation is given to us, and we must decide what to do with it. In the same way, everything you have read so far in this book is a seed, and it will be your decision what to do with it.

We can get to our house, put them in a jar with a cotton ball and water, and take care of them every day so that they begin to germinate, or we can forget them in the bottom of the bag or in the pants we were wearing that day and see how our marriage is lost in the ravages of the storms.

Every word of life sown in us represents one of these seeds.

Our marriage, which had begun to germinate like a bean in cotton, needed a lot of care so that it would not die. When germinating a plant, if we spend a day without pouring water or throwing too much on it, our little shoot can die of thirst or drown.

This is when we learn to converse with the Father like little children, not knowing what to say. At the same time, we must be very careful that no religious structure with laws and false doctrines comes and drowns our shoot. In the same way, in our marriage, we must speak to each other with care and love, with tact and esteeming the other as a very precious vessel, learning to communicate with the other, taking care of the structures that we already destroyed and that we do not want to forge again.

The Father worked a lot in my husband and me, and when we entered His order and got married, the transformation became even stronger. We nourish our little plants daily, reading his word together daily.

Little by little, we realized that the more time we spent with the Father, the stronger our little plant became, so we began to frequently seek a deeper relationship with Him.

As in any garden, the keeper must always unroot weeds that threaten the planting and watch for pests that could destroy it. It is time to become aware of the bad seeds that are part of our history and uproot them one by one. We must also take care of the influences in our environment that may be harmful, and that can activate harmful behaviors for one of the two.

These fasts bring with them a strong presence and anointing of God that serve as fertilizer to the little plant (our marriage) that has ceased to be a sprout, developed a stem and leaves, and is growing happily in its pot.

And as Jesus said, only one in four will take the time to do this work.

> " Then He spoke many things to them in parables, saying: "Behold, a sower went out to sow. And as he sowed, some seed fell by the wayside; and the birds came and devoured them. Some fell on stony places, where they did not have much earth; and they immediately sprang up because they had no depth of earth. But when the sun was up they were scorched, and because they had no root they withered away. And some fell among thorns, and the thorns sprang up and choked them. But others fell on good ground and yielded a crop: some a hundredfold, some sixty, some thirty."
>
> **Matthew 13:3-8**

We must take responsibility for our seeds. This is the point where most marriages are lost. People call a ministry and send messages asking for help, prayer, and deliverance. They genuinely do not understand why they cannot move forward in their spiritual life and marriage.

This work is a process that each of you must go through, and no one can do it for you; it is the responsibility of each one of you. BOTH must do it.

Now, this little plant, which represents our marriage in God, began to not fit in its pot, and a decision had to be made:

If we left that plant in the pot and gave it water daily, it wouldn't die. But we also knew that if that little plant weren't transplanted, it wouldn't grow any bigger.

My dear brethren, the church is full of potted, dependent, fragile, and disposable marriages. To have a kingdom marriage, we must transplant ourselves into the garden. What does this mean?

This implies taking things deep, not settling for easy, and passing solutions that produce only a moment of solace amid our struggles and storms. It requires a commitment on both sides to review the depths of hearts and bring out all that is and will be a hindrance to a married life immersed in the glory of God.

A pot is a relationship that is maintained on the surface. They try to get along well, to be accepted and seen as a good marriage in society and the church. Everything relevant, the internal ruptures, the failures that do not want anyone to know they exist, are only buried, and they are pushed deeper and deeper each time. This is how most couples live, avoiding confrontations or being exposed to shame. Ruled by the fear of being discovered or mistreated. Fleeing to false and sinful solutions. Hidden behind costumes that they do not even want to wear, but they have no other way to show their face.

Fear is a ruler that controls, enslaves, and destroys any relationship. Pot plants end up being like bonsai trees. Even if we cut off their life, destiny, and greatness, they must look pretty.

The garden is the freedom of two souls who dared to see themselves naked because love was greater than shame. Humility, courage, and the willingness to overcome at all costs in marriage are greater than pride and hypocrisy.

The garden is the territory where God and the couple live together. Where there is only light, life, and love.

" If we say that we have fellowship with Him, and walk in darkness, we lie and do not practice the truth. But if we walk in the light as He is in the light, we have fellowship with one another, and the blood of Jesus Christ His Son cleanses us from all sin. If we say that we have no sin, we deceive ourselves, and the truth is not in us. If we confess our sins, He is faithful and just to forgive us our sins and to cleanse us from all unrighteousness. If we say that we have not sinned, we make Him a liar, and His word is not in us.

1 John 1:6-10

This is where the great difference lies between the true leaders of light, the generation of resurrection and life, and the marriages willing to enter Eden:

Some will say, "Yes, I want", but they will not uproot iniquity in its depth; they will remove what is above, and the result will be that sooner rather than later, their plants or marriages will die because they did not take the time to deal with it.

One day, they will wake up, see everything dead, and ask the Father why. Until we are cleansed from all iniquity, we cannot enter the ways of the garden, much less the design of Eden.

Others are going to get to the bottom of it. So, persevere until everything is exposed to the light.

The love of the Father, the precious Blood of Jesus, and the Holy Spirit will accompany you in every millimeter of soil, in every tunnel of the dark caves of the heart and give you the tools you need to destroy every bad root and every weed.

We cannot advance in the Kingdom without going through this process. We can have a marriage, a little plant in a pot that will never grow or bear fruit. But if we want to move forward, this plant needs to be transplanted from the surface to the depth, from the natural to the supernatural. So that it may now live in the land of the garden, it must be cleaned, mineralized with the word and revelation that come directly from the Father, so that it is ready for sowing; so that marriage may be rooted in the principles and freedom of pure hearts.

And then the garden begins to grow.

> *"Then the Lord God took [a]the man and put him in the garden of Eden to [b]tend and keep it."*
> **Genesis 2:15**

Every word that comes from God is a plant that He sows in our garden. In the beginning, Eden was the sum of the Creator's thoughts materialized in all creation.

With time, you will begin to see all kinds of plants and trees in your garden, even entire forests, full of Our Father's mysteries and glorious wisdom.

Something that we must always be very aware of and attentive to is pulling out any bad weed that threatens the life of the plants in our garden. Remember, our job is to guard it.

The weeds that come from the world are, on the one hand, the product of our sin and the areas of our personality that we need to change, and, on the other hand, negative ideas contrary to our victory in Christ, which we must resist and tear from us. The first, we overcome on our knees, and the latter by believing in the truth.

If we let the weed multiply in our garden, it can be destroyed. That covetable fruit that invites us to eat it will invariably cause us to be expelled from the garden.

Other marriages or orchards will be abandoned by laziness, disorder, and neglect. When, instead of being watered by Christ, we try to do everything with our strength, we invariably end up tired and without wanting anything.

Our marriage planted in the garden must be cared for every day.

Thus, as it was in the beginning, the Father is in the garden waiting for you with joy EVERY DAY.

> *"And they heard the sound of the*
> *Lord God walking in the garden in*
> *the cool of the day"*
>
> **Genesis 3:8**

With Christ's resurrection, the heavens and the earth have been united, and we can live again in the Garden of Eden. That spiritual dimension is where God is walking with us, and we can talk to Him and share with Him.

Every day, with every sunrise, we have the choice to eat from the Tree of the Knowledge of Good and Evil or the Tree of Life within the Garden of Eden to worship God.

Jesus is the life that waters the garden of our marriage with his love and his word.

If we dedicate our lives to caring for our marriage in the garden, to walking in Eden with our Creator, we will need absolutely nothing, and every provision will be given to us..

> *"Out of the garden, we have to till the land from which we were taken."*

Genesis 3:23 Paraphrased

Outside the garden, there is sweat from work and effort; there is pain and subjugation; there is tyranny and injustice, misunderstanding, judgment, and violence. In short, outside the garden, there is darkness and death.

The most fascinating thing about the garden is that we let ourselves be surprised by something new and majestic that He will put in it every day. We can see how every word the Lord puts in our hearts begins to grow into a great forest. One filled with his presence, with portals that allow us to access eternal dimensions. A forest with deep-rooted oaks and crowns so high that they caress eternal dimensions.

A marriage in the garden is fruitful. And what is this fruit like?

Life manifests in this couple, where both are edified, seeking the cleansing of their hearts, abiding in holiness, and abiding in Christ above all else.

It is a marriage free of dogmas and subjugating doctrines, which lets out the light of Christ that clothes them because He Himself is their heavenly garments.

This fruit multiplies in their family, social, and work circles because the light and revival it radiates is so great, and everyone around them wonders: What is going on?

If your marriage does not produce the fruit of life, it is bearing that of death. You may project to be a beautiful Christian marriage, but people are impacted by the invisible that emanates from you, which has no words or appearances. Without doctrines, great words, or far-fetched sermons, that is what we impart into the world around us. Maybe it's time to see what WORD and seeds you are sowing in your garden.

If the sprouts do not come from the Word of the Father, set them on fire on your knees and start again. Tearing out now your sins, your idolatry of man, and all that does not come from God. If you do not burn them to the root, the consequences will be much worse.

The Father always lets you see the condition of your garden. It is time for humility, to face these conditions, and to ask for forgiveness. Lest we leave our Father alone, waiting for us in the Garden.

If your seed supplier is to go to a Pastor for a bean once a week, that will be your result. If a man is your seed provider because you have been told that his garden is fruitful, you will receive seeds that will be wonderful, and there will be others that may not be so wonderful.

But if your seed provider is the Father in the Garden of Eden, you will discover never-before-seen plants and animals. Deep forests and meadows are where the Holy Spirit runs, and His presence is breathed. It is entering into silence and stillness of soul and mind that God gives us these encounters. After you've been there, nothing will ever make sense again without Him.

Because it is there, in the same Eden, where you can see the origin of everything, which is from the very heart of the Father. Then you will rejoice in knowing that one day you will return there, not only in spirit but with your whole being. In that place, there is no longer any fear of death; there reigns the life and resurrection of Christ.

> *"The disciples say to Jesus, 'Tell us how our end will be.*

Jesus has said: Have you discovered, then, the beginning that you look for the end? For where the beginning is, there will be the end. Blessed is he who will take his place in the beginning; he will know the end and not experience death."

The Gospel of Thomas, verse 18

Here on earth, everything is transient, including who we are and what we have. When we arrive in this dimension, we forget Him. Only the pure in heart can access God's dimensions, those who are not lukewarm, those who do not conform to the worldly and religious systems, and those who do not wait to depart from this world to see Him. They love Him beyond their limits, wanting to understand every inch of His wisdom and Kingdom.

What a joy to walk through our garden and see how, as our marriage grows, the Father is sending us friends, companions, and brothers so that together, we may delight in seeing from the greatest to the smallest saplings of new revelations He gives us.

What a joy to feel God's glory walking in the morning clearing. Nothing comes close to the greatness of His Kingdom.

The Father originally placed us here in this garden so that we would take care of it and rule from it in oneness.

So, it's time for you to decide what you will do.

Clear the ground?

Are you ready to see the seeds germinate and start watching the garden grow?

Or will you stay in a "potted" marriage by the window?

Or worse, you're going to buy a plastic plant that looks green, doesn't need any care, doesn't need anyone, and is completely dead.

" For as the heavens are higher than the earth,
So are My ways higher than your ways,
And My thoughts than your thoughts."

"For as the rain comes down, and the snow from heaven,
And do not return there,
But water the earth,
And make it bring forth and bud,
That it may give seed to the sower
And bread to the eater

*So shall My word be that goes forth
from My mouth;*

*It shall not return to Me [a]void,But it
shall accomplish what I please,
And it shall prosper in the thing for
which I sent it."*

Isaiah 55: 9-11

Nothing fills our Father with joy more than a marriage like the one He created, in oneness with Him, in Eden.

We must have seeds that give us daily food and constantly sow so we never lack.

*"He answered and said, It is written,
Man shall not live by bread alone, but
by every word that proceeded from the
mouth of God."*

Matthew 4:4

Other seeds will grow into shrubs that will give us little sweet fruits, reminding us every day that He is here, in us, and delights in the joy and love of His children.

Words or seeds will also become trees in our garden; those are deep and high revelations.

I must also tell you that there are many heavenly gardens, but only true children of the resurrection can experience celestial marriage in the Garden of Eden.

A CALM
SEA

If we could learn anything from our storm, it is that love is not a feeling, not an exciting and passing feeling. Love is a daily commitment. It is Jesus himself living through us and discovering in the other the very essence with which he came out of the heart of God—that which is pure, without soulful buildings, without decorations of the world, that which is free of circumstances and consequences.

To discover that divine particle, we must discover its languages. In his wonderful book *"The Five Love Languages"*, Gary Chapman describes how love communicates.

1. Words of Affirmation
2. Quality time
3. Acts of service
4. Gifts
5. Physical contact

As he himself describes, each person tends to express and receive love differently. If you and your spouse know each other's language, you can communicate your love so that you and your beloved feel loved and that "the gas tank of love," as he describes it, stays full. This is a book that I recommend reading to all marriages.

Each relationship is unique in its virtues and geniuses, as well as in its defects and things that we do not like, and these combinations make each marriage unique and unrepeatable. On the other hand, some things are the foundations of life and love within that unique being.

"And though I bestow all my goods to feed the poor and give my body [a]to be burned, but have not love, it profits me nothing. Love suffers long and is kind; love does not envy; love does not parade itself, is not puffed up; does not behave rudely, does not seek its own, is not provoked, thinks no evil; does not rejoice in iniquity, but rejoices in the truth; bears all things, believes all things, hopes all things, endures all things.

1 Corinthians 13:3-7

"I charged you," he said, "in my first commandment to keep faith and fear and temperance." "Yes, sir," I said. "But now," he insisted, "I want to show you their powers as well, so that you can understand what the power and effect of each of them is. Because its effects are twofold and refer to both the just and the unjust. Therefore, you trust in justice, but do not trust in injustice; For the path of justice is narrow, but the path of injustice is crooked. But walk on the narrow [and flat] path and leave the crooked. For the crooked road has no clear paths, but places without a

marked path, it has stones to stumble on, and it is rough and full of thorns. Thus, it is detrimental to those who walk in it. But those who walk on the straight way, walk on flat ground and without stumbling: for it is neither rough nor thorns. You see, therefore, that it is more expedient to walk on this path." "I'm glad, sir," I said, "to walk this path." "You shall walk, yes," he said, "and whoever turns to the Lord wholeheartedly shall walk in him."

Shepherd of Hermas (Apocrypha)
Sixth Mandate

Let us, therefore, walk in our marriage on the straight road, on the flat road, in which it is not rough nor has thorns. Let us make our union our resting place, where we can live in the wonderful "Movement at Rest" in Christ.

"Jesus said, 'If they say to you' 'Where did you come from?' say to them, 'We came from the light, the place where the light came into being on its own accord and established <itself>, and became manifest through their image. If they say to you 'Is it you?' say, 'We are its children, and we are the elect of

*the living Father' If they ask you "What
is the sign of your Father in you?" tell
them "It is movement and repose."*

Gospel of Thomas verse 50

That place where there will be good days and others not so good, but where we know that, when we get home, we will find a refuge, we will find our unity, so that together we rest in Christ because we know who we are, where we come from, and in whom we rest.

Take the time to look into each other's eyes, hug each other, breathe together, and see yourselves inside.

Discover the essence of the other. It never ceases to amaze me every time I find a new look or priceless jewelry inside my husband's heart, and I feel more fortunate and prouder of him every day. Not only for overcoming addictions, but for the humility I see in him daily. I am moved by how he gives his will to the Lord to continue the straight path, plain and without stumbling, one day at a time and with Jesus by the hand. His victory, he does not take for granted; he conquers it daily.

I marvel at discovering in him the joy of the Father. He is always creative and can make us laugh, even in the most unlikely situations.

Matthew 19:14 says, *"Then Jesus said, 'Let the children come to me. Do not hinder them, for the kingdom of heaven belongs to those who are like them."*

These words perfectly describe my husband's soul and spirit, his innocence and mercy, and the strength they bring within. These qualities have brought us to safety in every storm that looms on the horizon, threatening our ship.

> *And he said to me, 'Keep simplicity and innocence, and you will be like a little child, who knows not the wickedness that destroys the lives of men.'*
>
> **Pastor of Hermas Second Term**

Whether someone has hurt or betrayed him, he always finds a word of prayer and mercy for them. Every day, I admire his temperance, his "left hand," as he says, which invariably leads him to bring out the best in the people with whom he interacts.

This ability to see beyond inside people makes him connect with the essence of them, whether they are the homeless with whom he talks on the street or entrepreneurs and leaders from all walks of life. No matter who it is, he always treats them like a real brother.

At home, he is the mast that holds the sails; the rudder was long ago left to Christ. He is that column where we can all come to embrace each other and where together we can drop anchor when we need it. His steadfastness inspires us to spread the sails that have taken us to the most wonderful places in God's heart.

It never ceases to amaze me how, from that mast, like a sentinel, he observes and cares for everyone around him; his heart, full of mercy, always tries to ensure that everyone is well. If someone needs something, he is the first to jump to help, to be, to serve as necessary. Even things as small as leaving the house and returning with a piece of chocolate that silently comes full of an "I'm thinking of you."

Our life is a constant gratitude for all that we have and all that we do not have. There is not a day that I do not embrace Him or thank God for allowing me to experience His love through Him and how fortunate I am to **be one being** with Him.

Recently, while studying the astronomical secrets in the Book of Enoch chapter 41, something moved everything inside me because I identified myself completely. It says:

"And I saw the chambers of the sun and the moon, whence they come from, and where they return, and their glorious return, and how one is superior to the other, and their majestic orbit, and how they leave their orbit, and add nothing to their orbit or take anything away from it, and remain faithful to one another, according to the oath by which they are united."

> *"And they give thanks and praise and do not rest;" "For them to thank is to enter into their rest."*

We remain faithful to one another according to the oath by which we are united, and every time we give thanks, we enter the rest of the Father. So, you don't have to complicate your life too much. Do you want to enter God's rest? Be thankful.

In our marriage, we live in constant thanksgiving, and thus, we enter the rest of the Father.

We learned to tell each other what we do not like about each other with love, and if one of us is wrong, to ask for forgiveness and work in that area to continue growing in love.

So, enjoy the journey, sail in love in His waters of life, and immerse yourself in the dimensions of His garden in Eden. Let yourselves be surprised by the Father, discover together the joy of life, and impact with the light of the resurrection that lives in you, all those around you. Do not complicate life. Being happy is simple.

We can change the world one marriage at a time, bring the light and gospel of Jesus to the whole planet, and reign in the design in which we were created, living in Him and with Him.

Giving to our Father always, all the glory and all the honor forever and ever.

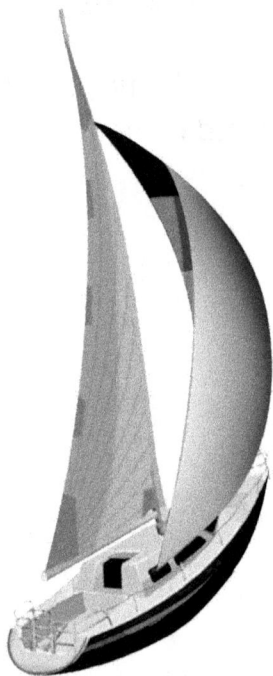

• L. Emerson Ferrell, "The Resurrection Generation" (2021) VOTLM

• Bible Dictionary, The Treasury of Knowledge, estudiosbiblicos.org

• Gordon Fee. First epistle to the Corinthians. New Creation. Buenos Aires. 1994. 569-572

•Harrison, E. F., Bromiley, G. W., & Henry, C. F. H. (2006). Dictionary of Theology (93). Grand Rapids, MI: Challenge Books.

• Douglas, J. (2000). New Bible Dictionary, First Edition. Miami: United Bible Societies.

• A, Méndez Ferrell, S. Aquino, A. Louceiro Plattner, L. Méndez. "Gospel of Thomas" (2023) VOTLM

• (1), (2) A. Méndez Ferrell "The Spirit of Man" (2014) VOTLM pages 153-154

• G. Chapman "The 5 languages of love, The secret of love that endures"

• Shepherd of Hermas, online version

• Anonymous, "The Book of Enoch"

bibliography

www.ingramcontent.com/pod-product-compliance
Lightning Source LLC
Chambersburg PA
CBHW052041090426
42739CB00010B/2001